I Can't Believe It's Not Fattening!

I Can't Believe It's Not Fattening!

Over 150 Ridiculously Easy Recipes for the Super Busy

Devin Alexander

broadway books
New York

Library of Congress Cataloging-in-Publication Data
   Alexander, Devin.
   [I'm too busy to cook cookbook]
   I can't believe it's not fattening!: over 150 ridiculously easy recipes
for the super busy.
      p. cm.
   Includes index
   1. Reducing diets—Recipes. 2. Quick and easy cookery. I. Title. II. I'm
too busy to cook cookbook.

   RM222.2.A3792 2010
   641.5'635—dc22

                      2009018861

978-0-7679-3157-1

Printed in the United States of America

Book design by Elizabeth Rendfleisch
Photographs by Theresa Raffetto
Food styling by Jessica Gorman
Prop styling by Karin Olsen

10 9 8 7 6 5 4 3 2 1

First Edition

This book is dedicated to my dad, Ben Simone,

in the hopes that Mom will find the recipes in this book

easy enough and quick enough to make at least one new

one every night!

And for being a spectacular example of

how to be a business owner, while teaching me to

"Keep on Keeping On" . . . no matter what!

contents

ACKNOWLEDGMENTS

Some days I wake up and have to pinch myself—I went from being the fat girl who was picked on in high school to a career woman who gets to "play with" (and enjoy) food all day long while working with a group of insanely talented, committed people:

The whole crew at Broadway: my esteemed editor, Annie Chagnot; designer, Elizabeth Rendfleisch; and Tammy Blake, publicist extraordinaire. They've made this process effortless.

Stephanie Farrell, also known as the Test Kitchen Goddess, who has been my right-hand gal for years. Recipe tester Angela Nehmans, who manages to work her breaks around my books, playing a huge role in keeping me sane. Recipe testers Sandy Levin, Tessa Genchi, Lisa Cohen, Kathryn Jacoby, and Elizabeth Packer, who made numerous sacrifices for the cause. And "Super Mom" Heather Haque, who's selflessly and substantially assisted with my every undertaking since college.

My manager, Julie Carson May, and publicists, Jim Eber, Mary Lengle, Carrie Simons, and Ashley Sandberg, who've made me appear "everywhere out of nowhere" and who I'm also lucky enough to call friends.

My friends John Baker, Rasha Chapman, Alyssa Devore, Steve Farrell, Kelly Frazier, Heather and Tas Haque, Sandy Levin, Michelle Miller, Jamie Nehasil, Chris Nielsen, Nick Nunez, Kristine Oller, Amanda Philipson, Dawn Sostrin, and Jerry Whitworth, who offer never-ending support (and/or their tastebuds).

The team at Meyer Corporation, which keeps me well stocked with Circulon, the best nonstick cookware and bakeware. And the team at Heinz, which makes sure I have Smart Ones on hand when even ridiculously easy isn't good enough!

Photographer Theresa Raffetto and food stylist Jessica Gordon.

My entire family, who gives me the utmost in support—special thanks to my mom for testing many of the recipes. And last but not least, Jon Shafer, who sends the perfect number of text messages to keep a smile on my face even when things get as hectic as can be.

introduction

"*T*wenty minutes in your kitchen can save you three hours on a tread-mill."

Since you're holding this book, there's a good chance you've heard me say that. That's because I say it all of the time. Heck, I've even been quoted in the *New York Times* saying it. That's because it's my reality . . . and my saving grace. I was on the yo-yo diet fast track, gaining ten to fifteen pounds per year without fail from the time I was eight until I was fifteen. At that point, I tipped the scales at close to 190 pounds and was wondering why I could succeed at everything I put my mind to except losing weight. Then I heard that if you cut just 100 calories from your diet each day, on average, you'll lose ten pounds in a year. That really clicked. I immediately called upon the cooking skills my Italian grandmother be-stowed on me. The next thing I knew, I was actually losing weight—and, more importantly, keeping it off! All I did at that time was make minor tweaks to the foods I was already eat-ing. I'd make chicken Parmesan with full-fat cheese and full-fat sauce, but I wouldn't deep-fry the chicken. I'd use 2 teaspoons less mayonnaise when making a sandwich. Or I'd use a leaner cut of beef when making my favorite meatballs. Close to twenty years later, I live and breathe by cooking because it allows me to eat incredibly decadent food and enjoy all of the flavors I crave—guilt free.

Though I've lost over fifty-five pounds, I really don't struggle with my weight any more . . . well, unless you count that nagging five to ten pounds all women fluctuate, wishing they would conquer forever. But even with that, my weight is no longer the obsession it was for the first twenty-six years of my life. That's because I can eat all of the foods I love.

When I was on my book tour for *The Most Decadent Diet Ever!* I had my first and only very real reminder over the past ten years of what it was like to struggle and why cooking has truly transformed my life and even my happiness.

I left my home in Los Angeles and went on the road for thirty-seven days, launching the book on the *Today* show. Then I proceeded to travel around the country doing TV appearances, numerous book signings, and even in-person appearances for *Self* magazine's "Workout in the Park" series. Every day was packed, and I was on a train or plane over half of the days I was gone. This meant I had to rely on restaurants and airport food. Now we've all seen episodes of *The Biggest Loser* where the trainers tell the contestants how to order out. And we've all seen segments of the *Today* show and *Good Morning America* where a nutritionist comes on and tells us what to choose. But did you ever notice it's always the stuff you don't want? Sure, I can eat baked chicken and steamed broccoli and not do too too much damage. I can get a salad and skip the dressing and the cheese and everything else that might make it taste remotely palatable. Or I can get an egg-white omelet with veggies and choke it down and I won't gain the fifty-five pounds back. But where's the decadence in that?

Tried and true, I'm a food lover. I have cravings. And I have zero willpower. So I can play along with the nutritionist who tells me to eat the egg-white omelet with no goat cheese, but what she's not telling me (though I do know, having attended culinary school and worked in restaurant kitchens) is that there's a high likelihood that even if I do order that bland omelet, it's going to be prepared in way too much butter.

Think about it. If you go to a restaurant and your food doesn't arrive on the table in a timely manner or doesn't look good, you're not likely to return. And most restaurants don't even own nonstick pans, so they have no choice but to load the pan with butter or lard or some sort of fat so your omelet cooks quickly and without looking like a disaster that was scraped from the bottom of a pan. So instead of eating a Cheese & Olive Omelet (see page 28) made with 4 egg whites for only 154 calories and 5 grams of fat, I'm stuck eating a veggie omelet that has more fat and calories from the butter alone. If I'd made my omelet at home in less than ten minutes, I would have easily saved a couple hundred calories (not to mention plenty of cash!). Multiply that by a few meals a day, and you're needing a lot less cardio to keep your figure and your health.

But getting back to my trip. I travel a lot, and I'm used to facing bland options when I'm on the road. Fine. A couple days here or there eating plain food isn't going to kill me, trip my internal wiring, or set off what I call "danger-zone cravings." But, I noticed, being that this trip was longer than most, I got ridiculously tired of eating the same "safe" dishes over and over. I started having insane cravings the way I did when I was yo-yo dieting. It was horrible. I'd find myself in my hotel room at night calling the front desk to have the mini-bar removed, all the while plotting where I could find something to satisfy my choco-late craving that wouldn't totally make me gain weight. I had to wear my "tight jeans" the whole second half of the trip, even though they weren't comfortable for travel, so I would have a constant reminder that I couldn't eat the horrible airplane cookies even though they seemed tempting when I was restless at 30,000 feet with three hours to go.

I am fully aware that not everyone experiences cravings the way I do. For some, eating not-even-close-to-decadent foods all day wouldn't affect them at all at night. It wouldn't set off any triggers, and it wouldn't make them have nightmares about overeating. I'm also aware, based on my work with *The Biggest Loser* contestants, with my fans, and even many of my friends and colleagues, that I'm definitely not the only one. The obesity epidemic in America proves I'm not alone. And I contend that if people just cooked for themselves more often, they would struggle a lot less.

I often hear people say they don't have time to cook. But as I see it, we don't have time *not* to cook. Assuming the above is true—that twenty minutes in your kitchen can save you three hours at the gym—you're actually adding time to your life by cooking. Not only will you need to spend less time at the gym, you'll be shedding those unwanted pounds that are the direct cause of your spending way too much time in the doctor's office or waiting in line at the pharmacy to pick up your blood pressure or cholesterol medication or even in spending tons of time monitoring your sugar levels because of your Type 2 diabetes. And all of that costs money, which means you have to spend more time at work making the money to pay for it all. You also have to make more money to pay for the increased costs of your health insurance because of all of those doctor visits. As you can see, the cycle really is vicious.

So now you're thinking, oh, sure, it's easy for *you* to say. You know how to cook, you don't have three children, and you're not trying to work yourself out of debt. True, I'm not in debt and I don't have three children. But I do spend many stretches in my kitchen/office from 8:00 A.M. to 2:00 A.M. every day for weeks straight scurrying to get the next book out the door. And those stints are sandwiched between jaunts on the road. Plus, I'm stuck tast-ing food (and I'm surrounded by it) all day long to make sure the recipes are delicious by the time they get to you. And I only know how to cook because I learned. But it's really easy. It's truly like riding a bike. When you start, it's a bit shaky. You venture to the grocery store for the first time and you don't know that the chili garlic sauce is in aisle 4 and that there are better deals on the shrimp from the freezer. But you pick that up. Then you get in your kitchen and you have to clean the dust off the measuring cups, but that won't continue to happen either. It really does get easier and easier and . . . I promise.

So what are you waiting for? You can do this! You can be healthy, and you can love the food that gets you there. You just have to turn the page and pick up that spatula!

STREAMLINING FOR SPEED

Even with recipes as simple as the ones on these pages, there are always ways to stream-line your kitchen to make things even more convenient:

1. Cook in Bulk One or Two Nights per Week

Find dishes that you like that are versatile, and then make enough for the entire week. If you make Basic Grilled Chicken (see page 219), Brown Rice (see page 223), and so on, you'll be able to throw together meals quickly. Or boil some eggs (see page 224). Having prepared eggs on hand gives you a great go-to snack any time of day, and eggs are perfect as add-ins for salads and sandwiches. (Just be sure to stick to the egg whites!) Oatmeal is another great quick and healthy meal. Make a large container of oatmeal to last throughout the week, and store it in an airtight container in your refrigerator. Each morning add your favorite fruit, peanut butter, or even hot chocolate powder to give it an added kick!

I often recommend Sunday as a bulk cooking day. Throw in a roast that doesn't need watching while you do your laundry. You'll not only have dinner on Sunday evening, you'll also have plenty of scrumptious leftovers that set you up for success during the week.

2. Rely on Pre-cut, Pre-chopped Foods

This is a huge time-saving tip. It is unreal how many fruits, vegetables and even herbs now come already prepared and ready to use. Onions, carrots, mushrooms, melons, squash, ber-ries, and salad greens are often available in convenient, ready-to-go packages. And Garden Gourmet makes tubes of fresh herbs you can find in the refrigerated area of the produce section at your local grocery store, while Trader Joe's and a number of other markets stock frozen herbs. These products make measuring herbs a breeze and avoid time washing and chopping. True, these convenient foods are a bit pricier, but think of the expense as buying precious time in the kitchen. There is no price tag you can put on time available for family, friends, and much needed "you time."

Still not crazy about the idea of someone else washing and chopping your produce? Then do it yourself once or twice a week. Store your cut-up fruit in airtight plastic contain-ers to retain freshness and prevent vitamin loss. Place your washed and well-dried herbs and lettuces in veggie bags or bags with holes (to ensure circulation) or in open bags (in-stead of sealing them). For even better results, wrap the herbs and greens very loosely in paper towels before putting them in their bags (to trap excess moisture).

3. Befriend Your Butcher

There's no reason to spend hours at home trimming chicken breasts or filleting fish. Turn the butcher at your local grocery store into one of your secret kitchen shortcuts. At most grocery stores, it costs only a smile and a thank-you for the butcher to trim your meat, no matter the cut. When you arrive at the grocery store, go directly to the meat section. Pick out the packages of chicken, beef, pork, or seafood you want to buy, and ask your butcher to trim (and even portion) it for you, being very specific how you'd like it cut (you certainly don't want him to cut chicken breasts in half by filleting them if you need thick pieces). By the time you're finished shopping, your meat will be ready for you. At my grocery stores, the butchers, produce guys, fishmongers, and even most of the managers and cashiers know me by name . . . and not because I'm on TV. It's because I smile and say "hello" and "thank you." Not only are they open to giving me suggestions and going the extra mile to help me, but if the herbs look wilted or the fish doesn't look as fresh as I'd like, I ask if they have more in the back. When they do (which is often), they go get the good stuff for me.

4. Kill Cleanup with Parchment and/or Nonstick Aluminum Foil

If a recipe calls for a nonstick baking sheet, you can always line the sheet with nonstick aluminum foil (or parchment, if you're not cooking under the broiler). When the meal is cooked, all you do is throw away the foil and, voilà, your pan is clean. This is a particularly great tip for broiling. How many evenings have you spent scrubbing pans after a liquid was broiled onto them? Not my idea of convenient or fun.

5. Seek Out Sauces

Practically any meal can be kicked up by simply adding a low-fat sauce or fresh salsa. Don't be afraid to venture into the international foods section of your grocery store and do a little extra scoping through the produce section. You're likely to find some really great selections. A little bit of prepared sauce can sculpt that Basic Grilled Chicken (see page 219) or grilled salmon you made on Sunday into a different culinary adventure every night of the week. Just be sure to read labels and keep an eye out for sauces that are high in calories and sodium. Sometimes it's astonishing how much sodium a sauce packs.

6. Guesstimate Greens

With some ingredients, especially higher fat or calorie ones, you need to make sure you measure extremely accurately. With your greens, measurement is much less crucial because they pack so few calories. So save time by measuring them precisely once or twice, noting about how much of your handful a cup actually is. If you have large hands, a medium handful is likely to be about 1 cup. Smaller hands might need a bigger handful. Once you can associate a handful size to a cup size, you can eliminate the need to measure greens every single time. Plus you'll have one less cup to clean.

7. Stock Your Freezer

I've never been a big fan of freezing prepared meals. However, I swear by my freezer when it comes to keeping necessities like chicken breasts, fish, and shrimp on hand. Not only do they ensure I'll always have healthy options available even when I don't have time to make it to the grocery store, they also save me *lots* of money. I buy in bulk when otherwise pricey items go on sale, and then I never have to pay top dollar. Please note that buying prefrozen chicken breasts is not the same as buying fresh and freezing them yourself. If you buy "fresh" from the grocery store, chances are it's been frozen and defrosted already. If you freeze it, it's been frozen twice and isn't likely to be the same quality as if you simply bought it frozen. As with all foods, you want to check the labels before you buy a new product. I've seen packages of frozen boneless, skinless chicken breasts with added fats. I'm always sure to buy the ones without added fats and recommend you do the same.

8. Stock Your Pantry with Staples

Having a few key ingredients always on hand makes for a fast and easy meal. Stock up on brown rice, whole-wheat, whole-grain, or fiber-enriched pastas, a variety of mustards, cans of tuna, lower-sodium broths and stocks, even lower-sodium tomato sauce and canned tomatoes, and so on. Another idea is to keep whole-wheat pizza dough in the freezer. Some grocery stores now carry prepared dough, or you can sometimes purchase it from your favorite mom-and-pop pizzeria (I buy mine at Trader Joe's). Pile the crust high with reduced-fat cheese and your favorite toppings for a convenient everyone-friendly meal.

You might also consider making a monthly (or even quarterly) excursion to a natural foods store to stock up, especially if there isn't one conveniently close to your home. You're apt to find a number of foods that aren't stocked at your traditional grocery store that make healthy eating even more decadent. If you take the family on a field trip of sorts, the kids can start understanding labels and basic nutrition as you explore.

9. Organize Your Cupboard

An organized kitchen makes for a fast and happy cooking experience. Take time to clean out and organize your kitchen cupboards, shelves, and pantry. You can cut five to ten minutes off your cooking time just by being able to get to your ingredients, mixing bowls, measuring cups, and spoons faster—not to mention you will save money. Knowing exactly what you already have in your kitchen keeps you from ending up with six boxes of low-fat graham crackers occupying needed space on your shelves.

10. Multiply the Measuring Cups

These days, you can buy measuring cups and measuring spoons for pennies. Sure, you can go to a high-end cooking store and spend a fortune on them, but they're often stocked at 99-cent type stores and other discount stores, which is great news because I recommend having two or three sets of each. If you have only one, you have to do a lot more washing and drying while you're cooking—you're instantly slowed if you use the teaspoon measure for vanilla extract or another liquid ingredient and then need it for baking soda or another dry ingredient and you don't have a second one standing by.

11. Use Knives to Slice Minutes in the Kitchen

You definitely don't have to spend a fortune on knives, but they do need to be good. Not only do sharp knives help prevent injury (did you know one of the most common emergency room visits outside of gang-related injury is because of people trying to cut bagels with dull knives?), they significantly *cut* (pun intended) your prep time. If your knives don't allow you to make a straight slice, or if you have to put a lot of muscle into cutting, it's time to replace them.

12. Chop Cooking Time with the Right Cutting Boards

It may seem like a little thing, but trust me, an inadequate work surface will make you a turtle in the kitchen. If you're trying to cut or slice on an uneven surface, you're not only increasing your risk of injury (a slipping knife) but also slowing yourself down. I recommend investing in one extra-large cutting board to use for most of your prep: chopping veggies, shredding cheese, slicing cooked meats, and so on. Use a smaller one to work with raw meats so you can simply throw it in your dishwasher when you're finished working with it.

13. Portion Out Ready-to-Eat Foods

It's easy to overindulge when we are unaware of the actual amount of food we are putting into our bodies. When we eat something our taste buds love, for some reason our brains can go on autopilot, making it harder to put down the fork. At the end of a meal, why not store leftovers in single-serving portions? Not only does this mean a healthy serving for the next time, but it also makes reheating convenient. This is a great snack strategy as well. Break down bags of chips, nuts, and dried fruits or boxes of crackers and cereals into single-serving portions in airtight containers or zip-top bags (just be sure to put them back in their original bag and seal that shut as well—many zip-top bags you purchase don't keep foods as fresh as the original packing will). Not only will you know exactly how much fat and how many calories are in each bag, but also it makes them easy to grab when you are on the go or to need to throw them into a lunch bag.

14. Stock Up on To-Go Containers.

Instead of hauling around containers only to spend tons of time cleaning them (or, worse, having them stack up in your car, awaiting cleaning), head to your local warehouse store and buy recyclable to-go containers. That way it's easy to carry your healthy foods or leftovers, and you can enjoy other parts of life when you're finished enjoying them.

15. Get Others Involved

Who says Mom or Dad has to do all the cooking? Get the kids involved! Not only will this save you time, you'll be bestowing important life skills on the little ones. Folks who are comfortable in the kitchen are always better off than folks who aren't. If you can't cook, you're stuck relying on restaurants or living on microwaveable foods. If you can cook, your options for decadence are truly endless.

NATURAL VERSUS ARTIFICIAL INGREDIENTS: THE PERPETUAL CONFLICT

My personality is such that I always want to make people happy. That's part of what I love about cooking. No matter what people want to eat, I can "love them" through food. This also means that when I was catering and cooking for celebrities, I'd completely rework my recipes or even create new ones to suit each individual's desires and cravings, whether I agreed with those desires and cravings (or even understood them) or not. I've made vegan menus, raw menus, organic menus, and I've made full-on meat-and-potato dishes followed by the richest chocolate cake that uses . . . dare I say it—tons of white sugar. I truly believe what is right for one person is not right for all.

I am a huge believer that it would be great if everything we put in our mouths was organic, natural, pure, unprocessed, untreated, *and* truly, 100 percent, inarguably good for us. Then the health-conscious, the ingredient hawks, and even the medical professionals would all be happy. Sadly, though, from where I'm sitting, right now this ideal is just that . . . an ideal.

Now I'm sure some people out there think it shouldn't just be an ideal—it should be the way it is. And I suspect most of those people are lucky enough not to experience the cravings I and so many of my clients, including *The Biggest Loser* contestants I've worked with, have. So instead of mandating that everything you eat is natural, I do my best to use as many whole ingredients as possible while adding slightly less natural ones when necessary in order to achieve maximum flavor.

Now if you're not on board with this philosophy and you're sitting there thinking, "No!

You can't call fat-free ice cream healthy, no matter what," consider this: what if your best friend or your teenage daughter weighed over 300 pounds and her weight struggle was greatly affecting her quality of life? At that weight, her health would most likely be at risk in various ways. But what if she could satisfy her sugar cravings by eating Broiled Peaches à la Mode (see page 195) instead of the peach pie à la mode she previously indulged in? And what if this recognition that there are better ways of eating enabled her to make changes that helped her in finally reaching a healthy weight and in feeling strong, powerful, and even have better self esteem? Granted, if all you eat is processed food and tons of chemicals, you're putting your health at risk no matter if you look fit or not. But for some, including myself, who do or have battled food, sometimes a small amount of artificial sweetener in the form of yogurt included in my baked goods doesn't seem totally evil. And for some people, having "just one tablespoon" of real whipped cream, as I've heard others suggest, is somewhat of an impossibility because once real whipped cream enters the house, it just somehow "disappears" or creates an obsession.

Now please don't get me wrong: I'm not trying to make a case for eating artificial ingredients. In fact, I think we should stay away from them when at all possible. But I also have enough experience with so many people's food quirks, cravings, and desires to understand that everyone really does have different needs. And the only person who can assess what's best for you is you . . . with a little help from your doctor, of course.

As you flip through these pages, I think you'll pretty quickly see a compromise of sorts. I incorporate many whole foods with nutritionally minded ingredients, from plenty of chicken breasts and brown rice to all-natural wing sauce, into healthy, decadent, and convenient dishes.

To that end, I've attempted to create a balanced selection throughout the book. A large percentage of the recipes can easily be made with 100 percent natural ingredients. I've also included a guide to tweaking the recipes that don't obviously have natural substitutions (see page 14). Plus, for many recipes, particularly where yogurt is used, I've provided nutritional information for the finished dishes if you choose natural yogurt (always higher in calories) and if you choose artificially sweetened yogurt (always lower in calories).

The most important thing for me (and so many others who have succeeded in gaining and maintaining health) is balance. For you, the key might be to stop striving for perfection by excluding every artificial ingredient from your diet all together, but instead, strike the right balance between the foods you believe are best for you *and* the foods that most greatly satisfy your cravings or even allow you to eat more volume (I'm a huge fan of this one). Or it might be to stick to natural ingredients even if that means that you must consume more calories or spend more money to do so. You just have to find out what works best for *you*.

UNDERSTANDING THE WORLD OF ORGANIC
AND ALL-NATURAL PRODUCTS

People (including me in the paragraphs that precede this) throw around the terms *natural* and *organic* a lot. And I talk throughout the book about the importance of reading labels. So I thought it might be helpful to provide a quick breakdown of what these terms mean to you as a consumer.

According to the latest definition from the U.S. Department of Agriculture (USDA):

> Organic food is produced by farmers who emphasize the use of renewable resources and the conservation of soil and water to enhance environmental quality for future generations. Organic meat, poultry, eggs, and dairy products come from animals that are given no antibiotics or growth hormones. Organic food is produced without using most conventional pesticides; petroleum-based fertilizers or sewage sludge-based fertilizers; bio-engineering; or ionizing radiation. Before a product can be labeled "organic," a Government-approved certifier inspects the farm where the food is grown to make sure the farmer is following all the rules necessary to meet USDA organic standards. Companies that handle or process organic food before it gets to your local supermarket or restaurant must be certified, too.

In addition to the USDA organic label, you might see different organic labels in grocery stores. That's because the United States recognizes three levels of organics:

1.   Products made entirely with certified organic ingredients and methods are labeled *100% organic*.

2.   Products made with at least 95% organic ingredients can be called *organic*. Products that fall into these two categories may display the USDA organic seal.

3.   The third category is for products containing a minimum of 70 percent organic ingredients, which may be labeled *made with organic ingredients*.

Admittedly, this stuff can get a little tricky, especially when talking about meat, eggs, dairy, and seafood. For meats to be organic, livestock must be fed *only* certified organic feed, may not be injected with hormones or antibiotics, and must have access to the outdoors, including pastureland for grazing. Dairy must come from livestock raised by the same standards. "All-natural" meat and dairy products are like organic meats, but they might not be fed organic feed exclusively. It's quite expensive for ranchers and farmers to feed their livestock 100 percent organic feed (even if they don't use hormones or antibiotics or adhere to other standards), which is why organic meat is often significantly more expensive than other meats. Organic eggs are available, but know that just because eggs are labeled vegetarian, cage-free, or free-range doesn't automatically qualify them as organic.

Now, is there such a thing as organic seafood? Most experts say no. You may see seafood labeled organic, but don't be fooled; the USDA does not put its "organic" stamp on seafood. If you see that label, it's from an independent or foreign agency. However, you *can* purchase wild-caught seafood, which means the fish is caught in its natural environment and did not come from a farm. Because wild-caught fish were able to swim freely, they are often leaner, with less fat and calories than farm-raised fish.

When you come across a label that reads *all-natural*, that means the final product was made solely from botanical resources without any use of additives or preservatives. The all-natural phenomenon has become popular in recent years because consumers can purchase products without additives that cost less than certified organic products.

You might be thinking to yourself, is it really worth the extra dollars and effort to eat organically? I think that decision is up to you, but many studies do show eating organic and all-natural products can be beneficial. I don't want to overwhelm you with too many statistics, but a recent study gives us pretty good evidence for the benefits of buying organic, especially when it comes to meats, dairy products, and produce (particularly produce with thin skin, like tomatoes and apples, as opposed to thicker-skinned produce, like pineapples and bananas). A four-year study conducted by the European Union found organic fruit and vegetables contain up to 40 percent more antioxidants and dairy up to 60 percent more than their conventionally produced counterparts. Though there isn't a ton of conclusive research on the benefits of eating organic and all-natural, it's safe to say that making an effort to eat fewer processed and chemically treated foods is definitely a good thing for all of us! The best advice I can give anyone looking to eat naturally or organically is to be informed and to read labels. Don't be fooled by phrases like *cage-free*, *made with natural ingredients*, or *made with organically grown*. . . . When you flip the package over and read the label, you may find the product in fact contains some all-natural or organic ingredients, but it may *also* contain additives, chemicals, or preservatives. You may end up spending extra for such products without getting the benefits of truly all-natural or organic items. Make sure you spend your hard-earned dollars on products you really want, not simply things marketed a certain way. And don't be fooled into thinking that just because a marinara sauce has a label that reads *100% organic and all-natural* that sauce is necessarily good for you. I've seen organic marinara sauces that have 14 grams of fat for a $1/2$-cup serving.

ALL-NATURAL RECIPES

The following recipes are either already written to be made with all-natural ingredients or can easily be tweaked to be made with them by following the simple guidelines on page 14.

Bring On the Breakfasts

Cheesy Breakfast Quesadilla with Fresh Salsa

Peppered Turkey & Egg Breakfast Sandwich

Cheddar Breakfast Wrap

Breakfast Pastrami Sandwich

Breakfast Fried Rice

Mini Frittatas with Herbed Goat Cheese

Cheese & Olive Omelet

Super-Cheesy Scrambled Eggs

Peanut Butter & Banana Waffle Sandwich

PB&J Oatmeal

Pomegranate Oatmeal

Chocolate Banana Breakfast Bowl

Chocolate Peanut Butter Breakfast Banana Split

Chocolate Raspberry Breakfast Sundae

Pineapple Coconut Breakfast Banana Split

Orange Chocolate Parfait

Raspberry Lemonade Smoothie

Apple Cinnamon (Breakfast) Bruschetta

Crunchy Breakfast Banana Logs

Better Burgers, Sandwiches, & Wraps

Drippin' Kickin' Burger

Blackened Salmon Sandwich

Turkey Provolone Toaster Sandwich

Santa Fe Chicken Melt with Guacamole

Fully Loaded Turkey Burrito Pocket

Southwest Chicken Open-Ended Wrap

Overstuffed Chicken Guacamole Wrap

Open-Ended BBQ Chicken Wrap

Amazing Appetizers & Savory Snacks

Enchizza

Rock & Roll Pizza Roll

Boneless Honey BBQ Wings

Asparagus Roast Beef Roll-Ups

Tuna Sashimi with Jalapeño

Garlic Cheese Breadsticks

A+ Apple Cheddar Skewers

Quick Crunchy Potato Chips

Fixed-Up French Onion Dip

Margarita Chips

Wow 'em White Bean Dip

Midsection-Melting Main Courses

Asian Grilled London Broil

Luau London Broil

Mexican Cocktail Meatballs

Easy-As-Can-Be Pot Roast Supper

Boneless Pork "Ribs"

Simple Glazed Pork Chops

ORGANIC & ALL-NATURAL SUBSTITUTIONS

For the most part, substituting all-natural and organic ingredients is pretty simple. Just look for labels that say *all-natural* or *organic*. Just be sure to note that, for example, organic chocolate syrup may have a few more calories than the traditional stuff. For the most common (but not quite so obvious) substitutions, I've created a chart to help you know which ingredients to buy if you want to go all-natural or organic.

If Recipe Calls for...	*Replace with...*
bacon, center-cut	organic or all-natural center-cut bacon; Applegate Farms makes both All-Natural Sunday Bacon and Organic Sunday Bacon with only 10 calories and 1 gram fat more per 2-slice serving than conventional center-cut bacon
butter-flavored cooking spray	100% canola oil spray
coconut, sweetened flake	organic coconut flakes (to date, I've only found unsweetened, however)
egg substitute	2 organic large egg whites per 1/4 cup egg substitute, or a 1:1 substitution of 100% liquid egg whites
goat cheese crumbles	log of all-natural or organic goat cheese, then crumble it yourself
meats (ground beef, London broil, top round steak, pork tenderloin, chicken breast, turkey cutlets)	certified organic or all-natural meats (be sure to read labels to ensure they are truly organic or all-natural)
mini chocolate chips	organic chocolate chips, chopped into small pieces

parmesan cheese, grated, reduced-fat	all-natural grated parmesan cheese, which has an additional 5 calories and 1 gram of fat per 5-gram (about 1 teaspoon) serving
pasta or macaroni, fiber-enriched	all-natural or organic whole-wheat or whole-grain pasta or macaroni
peppered turkey	another all-natural or organic meat, such as all-natural Canadian bacon, extra-lean ham, or smoked turkey
pierogies	all-natural pierogies. I found whole-grain pierogies: Living Right Natural Foods Multigrain Pierogies, which will add about 5 grams of fat per serving
roasted bell peppers	an all-natural or organic brand (such as Mediterranean Organics), or purchase raw organic bell peppers and roast them yourself
salt	all-natural sea salt
seafood (tilapia, salmon, shrimp)	wild-caught instead of farm-raised seafood (Note: most experts agree that truly organic seafood does not exist, so you probably won't find any seafood labeled *organic*.)
sugar, granulated	1:1 substitution of organic or all-natural raw sugar or organic or all-natural cane sugar (also called *evaporated cane juice*)
whipped topping, frozen	natural whipped topping, which will add at least 2 grams of fat per 2-tablespoon serving, depending on the brand (Tru-Whip makes one)
yogurt, artificially sweetened	organic naturally sweetened yogurt, which is about an additional 7 calories per ounce

TO MICROWAVE OR NOT TO MICROWAVE . . . THAT IS THE QUESTION

Let me remind you I'm not a doctor and I'm certainly not a scientist, so you might want to consider doing a little research on this topic on your own. I know tons of people use their microwave as a mainstay. Yet I occasionally receive letters from fans of *Healthy Decadence* asking that I don't use the microwave because their doctors have suggested they not use one.

I'm all about balance, as I mentioned above. I've found numerous pieces of research suggesting you should not put plastic in the microwave, so I make sure not to do that, and I've written the recipes in this book to support that. However, this is a book about convenience, and it doesn't seem that, as a society, we have thrown away our microwaves. The most convenient option in preparing most of the recipes is definitely to use the microwave. But I've also provided an alternative where possible so folks who choose not to use a microwave can still enjoy the dishes.

bring on the breakfasts

bacon & egg breakfast quesadilla

Hands-on Time: 10 MINUTES (MICROWAVE) OR 12 MINUTES (STOVETOP) •
Hands-off Time: NONE

Instead of slaving over a stove in the morning, buy packaged 50% reduced-fat bacon pieces. You'll save tons of time, and you'll be less likely to overindulge because you won't have the smell of bacon wafting through the house for hours.

Look for the bacon pieces near the croutons and other salad ingredients in your favorite grocery store. Or, if you love them as much as I do, head to Costco and buy them in a big bag. They keep fresh in the refrigerator for a long time.

Olive oil spray

3 large egg whites

1 (about 8-inch diameter) reduced-fat, whole-wheat flour tortilla

3/4 ounce (about 1/3 cup) finely shredded light Swiss cheese

1 tablespoon 50% less fat real bacon pieces (I used Hormel)

1 teaspoon finely chopped cilantro leaves, or more to taste (optional)

Microwave Instructions

Lightly mist a small, microwave-safe bowl with spray. Add the egg whites and microwave for 30 seconds on low. Continue microwaving them in 30-second intervals until they are just a bit runny on top. Then using a fork, stir them to break into large "scrambled" pieces. By the time you "scramble" and stir them, the residual heat should have cooked away the runniness. If they are still undercooked, cook them in 10-second intervals until just done.

Place a nonstick frying pan large enough for the tortilla to lie flat over medium-high heat. Add the tortilla (no need to add any fat). Sprinkle half the cheese over half the tortilla, followed by half the bacon. Spoon the egg evenly over the cheese and bacon, followed by the remaining cheese, bacon, and cilantro, if desired. Fold the bare half over the filled half. Cook for about 2 minutes, or until the cheese is beginning to melt and the tortilla is lightly browned in spots. Carefully flip the filled tortilla over and cook until the cheese is completely melted, 1 to 2 minutes. Transfer the quesadilla to a serving plate and cut it into 4 wedges. Serve immediately.

Stovetop Instructions

Follow the directions above, but instead of microwaving the egg whites, simply scramble them in a nonstick skillet lightly misted with spray over medium heat.

Makes 1 serving. 238 calories, 24 g protein, 24 g carbohydrates, 6 g fat, 2 g saturated fat, 18 mg cholesterol, 2 g fiber, 580 mg sodium

cheesy breakfast quesadilla
with fresh salsa

Hands-on Time: 10 MINUTES (MICROWAVE) OR 12 MINUTES (STOVETOP) • *Hands-off Time:* NONE

I love eating quesadillas for breakfast. They're a snap to throw together, yet they're a hot comfort food and a great start to your morning. The egg whites add plenty of lean protein to help keep you full and satisfied. For variety, I like to vary the kind of cheese I use.

Olive oil spray

4 large egg whites

1 (about 8-inch-diameter) reduced-fat, whole-wheat flour tortilla

1 ounce (1/3 cup) finely shredded light Swiss cheese

1/4 cup drained fresh salsa (refrigerated, not jarred, if possible)

Microwave Instructions

Lightly mist a small microwave-safe bowl with spray. Add the egg whites and microwave for 30 seconds on low. Continue microwaving them in 30-second intervals until they are just barely runny on top. Then using a fork, stir them to break into large "scrambled" pieces. By the time you "scramble" and stir them, the residual heat should have cooked away the runniness. If they are still undercooked, cook them in 10-second intervals until just done.

Place a nonstick frying pan large enough for the tortilla to lie flat over medium-high heat. Add the tortilla (no need to add any fat). Sprinkle half the cheese over half of the tortilla. Spoon the egg evenly over that, followed by the remaining cheese. Fold the bare half over the filled half. Cook until the cheese begins to melt and the tortilla is lightly browned in spots, about 2 minutes. Carefully flip it and cook until the cheese is completely melted, 1 to 2 minutes. Transfer the quesadilla to a serving plate and top with salsa. Cut into 4 wedges and serve immediately.

Stovetop Instructions

Follow the directions above, but instead of microwaving the egg whites, simply scramble them in a nonstick skillet lightly misted with spray over medium heat.

Makes 1 serving. 257 calories, 27 g protein, 28 g carbohydrates, 6 g fat, 2 g saturated fat, 10 mg cholesterol, 2 g fiber, 518 mg sodium

peppered turkey & egg breakfast sandwich

Hands-on Time: 4 MINUTES (MICROWAVE) OR 12 MINUTES (STOVETOP) • *Hands-off Time:* NONE

This sandwich is a convenient, even leaner twist on a more traditional Canadian bacon and egg breakfast sandwich I love. Feel free to swap in Canadian bacon, extra-lean smoked ham, or even light salami—it's delicious with any of them.

If you time it just right, the cheese will melt between the hot muffin and the hot egg. If that's too precise for you, you can wrap the sandwich in a paper towel and microwave it for 15 to 30 seconds on low power to melt the cheese completely. Just be careful not to overmicrowave it, or the English muffin will become chewy.

Olive oil spray
2 large egg whites
1 light multigrain English muffin
1 slice ($3/4$ ounce) 2% milk American cheese
1 ounce thinly sliced or shaved extra-lean deli peppered turkey

Microwave Instructions

Lightly mist a $3^{1}/2$ or 4-inch diameter ramekin or microwave-safe bowl with spray. Add the egg whites.

Toast the English muffin in a toaster or under the broiler.

Microwave the egg in 30-second intervals on low until it is no longer runny. Use a butter knife to loosen the egg "patty" from the ramekin. Assemble the sandwich by placing the bottom half of the English muffin, inside up, on a serving plate. Top it with the cheese, the egg, the turkey, and then the top half of the muffin. Serve immediately.

Oven Instructions

Follow the directions above, but instead of microwaving the egg whites, preheat the oven to 400°F. Place the ramekin of egg whites in a small baking dish or pan. Fill the dish with enough water to come halfway up the ramekin. Bake the egg whites for 18 to 20 minutes, or until just set.

Makes 1 sandwich. 205 calories, 23 g protein, 26 g carbohydrates, 5 g fat, 2 g saturated fat, 22 mg cholesterol, 8 g fiber, 774 mg sodium

cheddar breakfast wrap

Hands-on Time: 5 TO 7 MINUTES (MICROWAVE) OR 8 TO 10 MINUTES (STOVETOP) • *Hands-off Time:* NONE

I love changing this wrap by purchasing an assortment of tortillas; La Tortilla Factory makes excellent pumpernickel tortillas, while Tumaro's makes jalapeño and cilantro and even pesto varieties. Just be sure to read the labels. You don't want to accidentally grab one with an exorbitant amount of calories or fat.

Olive oil spray
4 large egg whites
1 (about 8-inch-diameter) reduced-fat,
    whole-wheat flour tortilla
1 ounce (about ½ cup) finely shredded 75%
    light Cheddar cheese (I used Cabot's)
2 tablespoons seeded and finely chopped
    tomato

Microwave Instructions

Place the tortilla on a microwave-safe plate between two damp paper towels.

Lightly mist a medium microwave-safe bowl with spray. Add the egg whites. Microwave the egg whites for 30 seconds on low. Continue microwaving them in 30-second intervals until they are just a bit runny on top. Then stir them with a fork, breaking them apart into large pieces. By the time you "scramble" and stir them, the residual heat should have cooked away the runniness. If they are still undercooked, microwave them in 10-second intervals until just done. Set aside.

Microwave the tortilla on high until warm, 10 to 20 seconds. Discard the paper towels and spoon the cooked eggs in a 3-inch-wide strip down the center of the tortilla, leaving 1 inch bare at each end of the strip. Top the eggs with the cheese, followed by the tomato. Fold the bare ends of the tortilla toward the center, and then roll the sides over the filling to form a burrito. Cut the wrap in half on an angle. Serve immediately.

Stovetop Instructions

Follow the directions above, but instead of heating the tortilla in the microwave, wrap it completely in foil, and then heat it in a 400°F oven for 4 to 5 minutes. And instead of microwaving the egg whites, simply scramble them in a nonstick skillet lightly misted with spray over medium heat.

Makes 1 serving. 241 calories, 27 g protein, 25 g carbohydrates, 5 g fat, 2 g saturated fat, 10 mg cholesterol, 2 g fiber, 560 mg sodium

breakfast pastrami sandwich

Hands-on Time: 4 MINUTES (MICROWAVE) OR 8 MINUTES (STOVETOP) •
Hands-off Time: NONE

If you time this so the eggs are cooked just as the toast is done, the cheese should melt, eliminating the need to microwave the whole sandwich.

Do note that if you're watching your sodium, you might want to indulge in this sandwich only on occasion. It is on the higher side, but still has only a fraction of the sodium you'd find in a similar restaurant sandwich.

Olive oil spray
2 large egg whites
2 slices rye bread, toasted
1 slice reduced-fat or light Swiss cheese, cut
    in half (I used Sargento)
2 ounces deli-thin 98% lean turkey pastrami

Microwave Instructions
Lightly mist a small microwave-safe bowl with spray. Add the egg whites and microwave for 30 seconds on low. Continue microwaving them in 30-second intervals until they are just barely runny on top. Then using a fork, stir to break them into large "scrambled" pieces.

If they are still undercooked, cook them in 10-second intervals until just done.

Place a piece of the toast on a serving plate and top it evenly with the cheese, followed by the eggs, then the pastrami. Top the sandwich with the remaining toast slice. Wrap it in a paper towel and microwave it on high for 10 seconds to warm it through. Serve immediately.

Stovetop Instructions
Follow the directions above, but instead of microwaving the egg whites, simply scramble them in a nonstick skillet lightly misted with spray over medium heat.

Makes 1 sandwich. 308 calories, 31 g protein, 30 g carbohydrates, 7 g fat, 2 g saturated fat, 37 mg cholesterol, 2 g fiber, 1,054 mg sodium

breakfast fried rice

Hands-on Time: 7 to 9 MINUTES • *Hands-off Time:* NONE

Years ago, I started making batches of short-grain brown rice over the weekend to use during the week. I always had it on hand to add to or accompany whatever I was cooking. This dish emerged as one of my regulars. It's easy and filling and an all-round great way to start any day.

If you don't want to make the rice in advance, don't worry. Fortunately, it's now easy to buy prepared brown rice either in the freezer section (you reheat it in the microwave) or even in the rice aisle. Just be sure to read the label—you don't want to buy a variety that contains added fats.

Olive oil spray

4 large egg whites

1/4 cup cooked brown rice (I prefer short-grain)

1/4 to 1/2 teaspoon chili garlic sauce (look for it in the international section, near the soy sauce)

1 tablespoon thinly sliced green onion tops, sliced on a diagonal

Salt and pepper, to taste

In a small bowl, using a fork or small whisk, whisk the egg whites until they bubble lightly.

Place a small nonstick skillet over medium heat. When warm, lightly mist the pan with spray and pour the egg whites into the pan. Using a wooden spoon, scramble the whites, allowing the uncooked egg whites to run underneath the pieces that begin to cook, for 3 to 5 minutes, or until almost set.

Stir in the rice, chili garlic sauce, and green onion. Continue stirring the mixture for another 1 to 2 minutes, or until the eggs are completely cooked and the ingredients are well combined. Season with salt and pepper and serve immediately.

Makes 1 serving. 123 calories, 16 g protein, 13 g carbohydrates, <1 g fat, trace saturated fat, 0 mg cholesterol, 1 g fiber, 242 mg sodium

mini frittatas with herbed goat cheese

Hands-on Time: 5 MINUTES •
Hands-off Time: TIME TO PREHEAT OVEN PLUS 15 TO 19 MINUTES

These frittatas are ridiculously easy, especially if you consider how elegant they look. I've served them numerous times to last-minute brunch guests . . . and on those mornings where I just needed a hot, high-protein breakfast without any fuss.

Do note it's important to let the frittatas rest a couple of minutes before serving. You need to give the egg a chance to set a bit before eating. Also, when crumbling goat cheese, it's best that it's cold (it's not a bad idea to freeze it slightly). When goat cheese is room temperature or only slightly chilled, it's softer and thus tends not to crumble well.

Also, 16 large egg whites or 2 cups 100% liquid egg whites can be swapped in for the egg substitute if preferred. Add 2 large egg whites or 1/4 cup 100% liquid egg whites to each cup of the muffin tin, and then follow the instructions below.

Olive oil spray
2 cups egg substitute
1 1/2 ounces herbed goat cheese, finely
   crumbled

Preheat the oven to 350°F. Lightly mist 8 cups of a nonstick, standard muffin tin with spray.

Pour the egg evenly among the prepared muffin cups, about 1/4 cup in each. Bake until almost set, 7 to 9 minutes. Sprinkle the goat cheese evenly over the tops, then continue baking for 8 to 10 minutes, or until the eggs are no longer runny and the cheese is slightly melted. Transfer the muffin tin to a cooling rack and allow the frittatas to set for 2 minutes. Using a butter knife, carefully lift the frittatas out of the tin and transfer them to serving plates. Serve immediately.

Makes 4 servings. Each (2-frittata) serving has: 89 calories, 14 g protein, 2 g carbohydrates, 2 g fat, 2 g saturated fat, 5 mg cholesterol, 0 g fiber, 289 mg sodium

cheese & olive omelet

Hands-on Time: 10 MINUTES • *Hands-off Time:* NONE

I love omelets, and this is one of my all-time favorites. Feel free to use any variety of olives here. No matter which you pick, you'll have a great result.

4 large egg whites
Black pepper, to taste
Olive oil spray
1¼ ounces (scant ½ cup) finely shredded reduced-fat mozzarella cheese (no more than 3 g of fat per ounce; I used Lucerne, found at Safeway chains)
1 tablespoon canned chopped black olives

Add the egg whites to a medium bowl and season them with pepper. Using a fork or small whisk, whisk them until the egg whites bubble lightly.

Place a medium nonstick skillet over medium heat. When warm, lightly mist the pan with spray and pour in the egg whites. Cook them, lifting the edges with a spatula as they start to set and tipping the pan for uncooked egg whites to run underneath, for 4 to 6 minutes, or until almost set. Flip the omelet. Add the mozzarella over half of the egg. Sprinkle the olives over the cheese. Flip the bare half over the filled half and continue cooking the omelet until the cheese is just melted, 1 to 2 minutes. Transfer to a serving plate. Serve immediately.

Makes 1 serving. 154 calories, 23 g protein, 3 g carbohydrates, 5 g fat, 1 g saturated fat, 13 mg cholesterol, <1 g fiber, 558 mg sodium

super-cheesy scrambled eggs

Hands-on Time: 4 MINUTES (MICROWAVE) OR 6 MINUTES (STOVETOP) •
Hands-off Time: NONE

When I was a kid, we always vacationed at the Jersey shore. Every summer we'd go to a fantastic little Italian restaurant. Not only did they have the most incredible rolls and meatballs, they had a fettuccine dish that was out of this world. Now I realize it was probably just pasta with tons of butter and tons of melted cheese. I loved it so much, but it probably contributed significantly to my weight gain.

When I threw this breakfast together one morning as I was running out the door, the gooey cheese surrounding the fluffy eggs reminded me of that fave from my past. But the good news is that this version won't cause nearly the damage.

Olive oil spray

4 large egg whites

1 ounce (about 1/4 cup) reduced-fat finely shredded Italian cheese blend or mozzarella cheese (I used Sargento Shredded Reduced-Fat Four-Cheese Italian Blend)

Pepper, to taste (optional)

Microwave Instructions

Lightly mist a small microwave-safe bowl with spray. Add the egg whites and microwave for 30 seconds on low. Continue microwaving them in 30-second intervals until they are just a bit runny on top. Then, using a fork, stir them to break into large "scrambled" pieces. By the time you "scramble" and stir them, the residual heat should have cooked away the runniness. If they are still undercooked, microwave them in 10-second intervals until no liquid remains.

Wait about 10 seconds after cooking to make sure the eggs are completely cooked and no moisture remains. Stir the cheese into the eggs until the cheese is well combined and melted. Season with pepper, if desired. Serve immediately.

Stovetop Instructions

Follow the directions above, but instead of microwaving the egg whites, simply scramble them in a nonstick skillet lightly misted with spray over medium heat.

Makes 1 serving. 147 calories, 23 g protein, 2 g carbohydrates, 5 g fat, 3 g saturated fat, 15 mg cholesterol, 0 g fiber, 445 mg sodium

peanut butter & banana
waffle sandwich

Hands-on Time: 4 MINUTES • *Hands-off Time:* NONE

This sandwich was actually the brainchild of my trainer, Brian, who eats it all the time. Make it for your kids before school, or for yourself when you want to add a little decadence to your morning. Heck, it's not only super tasty, it's trainer-approved.

2 low-fat whole-grain or whole-wheat waffles
   (140 calories or less per 2-waffle serving)
2 teaspoons all-natural creamy peanut butter
1/2 small banana, cut into 1/8-inch-thick slices

Toast the waffles according to package directions. Spread one side of each waffle with 1 teaspoon peanut butter. Top one waffle evenly with the banana slices, and then flip the other on top to make a sandwich. Serve immediately.

Makes 1 serving. 257 calories, 8 g protein, 42 g carbohydrates, 8 g fat, 1 g saturated fat, 0 mg cholesterol, 5 g fiber, 447 mg sodium

lemon poppy seed pancakes

Hands-on Time: 15 MINUTES (BATTER CAN BE PREPARED AHEAD) •
Hands-off Time: NONE

If eaten plain, these pancakes are a tad on the dry side, which is why I love to layer them with yogurt. The tartness of the lemon, paired with the creaminess of the yogurt and sweetness of the powdered sugar, transforms ordinary pancakes into a decadent, dessertlike breakfast.

Store the batter in a resealable plastic container in your fridge to have on hand. Note, however, that when the batter sits in the fridge, it will thicken slightly, so use a scant 1/4 cup batter per pancake to get 6 pancakes.

Another time-saving option is to freeze the cooked pancakes. To reheat frozen pancakes, microwave them in a single layer on high for 30 seconds to 1 minute, or until warmed through. Alternatively, place the pancakes on a nonstick baking sheet in a single layer. Cover the pan with foil and place in a 350°F oven for about 5 minutes, or until warmed through.

1 cup reduced-fat Bisquick
1 large egg white
3/4 cup fat-free milk
1/4 teaspoon lemon extract
1 teaspoon poppy seeds
Butter-flavored cooking spray
7 1/2 tablespoons fat-free lemon or lemon chiffon yogurt (not artificially sweetened), divided
3/4 teaspoon powdered sugar, divided

Preheat the oven to 200°F. In a small mixing bowl, whisk the Bisquick, egg white, milk, lemon extract, and poppy seeds until well combined.

Heat a large nonstick skillet over medium-high heat (see Note). When hot, lightly mist it with spray. Working in batches and respraying the pan between each, pour 1/4 cup per pancake of batter onto the skillet and let cook for 1 to 2 minutes, or until the pancakes have bubbles on the tops and the bottoms are golden brown. Flip the pancakes and continue cooking them until golden brown on the outside and cooked through, 1 to 2 minutes. Transfer the finished pancakes to an ovenproof plate, cover with foil, and keep them warm in the oven until they are all cooked.

Transfer one pancake to a serving plate. Top with 1 1/2 tablespoons yogurt, then another pancake and another tablespoon of yogurt. Sprinkle with 1/4 teaspoon powdered sugar. Repeat with the remaining pancakes, yogurt, and powdered sugar. Serve immediately.

NOTE If your pan gets too hot during cooking and the pancakes brown too fast, reduce the heat to medium so the outsides of the pancakes don't burn before the centers are done.

Makes 3 servings. Each (2-pancake) serving has: 215 calories, 8 g protein, 36 g carbohydrates, 4 g fat, <1 saturated fat, 2 mg cholesterol, <1 g fiber, 537 mg sodium

pb&j oatmeal

Hands-on Time: 3 MINUTES •
Hands-off Time: TIME TO BOIL WATER PLUS 10 to 12 MINUTES

What kid (big or small) doesn't love peanut butter and jelly? Well, here's an adult twist on the combination that incorporates all the health benefits of oatmeal and still allows you to enjoy this classic comfort combo. And the kids will love it, too!

1 cup water

Pinch salt

1/2 cup old-fashioned oats

2 teaspoons all-natural creamy peanut butter

1 1/2 tablespoons strawberry 100% fruit preserves

Combine the water and salt in a small non-stick saucepan. Place it over high heat and bring the mixture to a rapid boil. Add the oats and turn the heat to medium. Cook the oats 5 to 7 minutes, stirring occasionally, until the liquid is almost absorbed. Cover the pan and remove it from the heat. Allow it to sit 5 minutes, and then stir in the peanut butter and preserves. Serve immediately.

Makes 1 (about 1-cup) serving. 280 calories, 8 g protein, 44 g carbohydrates, 8 g fat, 1 g saturated fat, 0 mg cholesterol, 5 g fiber, 67 mg sodium

pomegranate oatmeal

Hands-on Time: 3 MINUTES •
Hands-off Time: TIME TO BOIL WATER PLUS 10 TO 12 MINUTES

In recent years, pomegranates have emerged as one of the healthiest fruits due to their power-ful antioxidants. Here's a quick spin on plain oatmeal you can enjoy for its delicious flavor while reaping the great benefits of this superfood.

$\frac{1}{2}$ cup water
$\frac{1}{2}$ cup 100% pomegranate juice
Pinch salt
$\frac{1}{2}$ cup old-fashioned oats
1 to 2 teaspoons brown sugar, not packed

Bring the water, juice, and salt to a rapid boil in a small saucepan over high heat. Add the oats and turn the heat to medium. Cook the oats 5 to 7 minutes, stirring occasionally, until the liquid is almost absorbed. Cover the pan and remove it from the heat. Allow it to sit 5 minutes, and then stir in the sugar. Serve immediately.

Makes 1 (scant 1-cup) serving. 231 calories, 8 g protein, 47 g carbohydrates, 3 g fat, 0 g saturated fat, 0 mg cholesterol, 4 g fiber, 89 mg sodium

burst of orange cream of wheat

Hands-on Time: 3 MINUTES • *Hands-off Time:* TIME TO BOIL ORANGE JUICE

We all need energy to start our days off right, and a healthy and hearty breakfast is the perfect way to do just that. When it comes to getting nutrition and satisfying early morning hunger, it doesn't get much better than this creamy cereal. You'll be shocked by how refreshing and rich this dish tastes. But in addition to being decadent, this breakfast is also packed with great nutrients like calcium, vitamin C, and iron.

1^1/4 cups 100% orange juice (not from concentrate, no pulp)

2 pinches salt

3 tablespoons Cream of Wheat Original 2^1/2 Minute Enriched Farina

^{1}/4 teaspoon vanilla extract

1 teaspoon brown sugar, packed

Bring the orange juice and salt to a boil in a small nonstick saucepan over high heat. Add the farina, stirring constantly until it's well blended. Reduce the heat to low. Simmer uncovered, stirring constantly, for about 2^1/2 minutes, or until the mixture thickens. Remove the pan from the heat and stir in the vanilla and sugar until well combined. Serve immediately.

Makes 1 serving. 291 calories, 3 g protein, 66 g carbohydrates, 0 g fat, 0 g saturated fat, 0 mg cholesterol, 1 g fiber, 232 mg sodium

chocolate banana breakfast bowl

Hands-on Time: 4 MINUTES • *Hands-off Time:* NONE

Anyone who knows me knows that although I've maintained a fifty-five-pound weight loss for close to twenty years, I proudly eat chocolate every day. Here's a great example of how I can face my chocolate craving head-on, even at breakfast!

1 medium banana, cut into 1/4-inch-thick rounds

1/2 cup Fiber One vanilla or naturally sweetened fat-free vanilla or banana yogurt

2 tablespoons low-fat granola without raisins

1 1/2 teaspoons chocolate syrup

Add the banana pieces to a small, deep bowl. Top them with the yogurt, then the granola. Drizzle the chocolate syrup on top. Serve immediately.

Makes 1 serving. Made with Fiber One yogurt: 268 calories, 6 g protein, 56 g carbohydrates, <1 g fat, trace saturated fat, 3 mg cholesterol, 10 g fiber, 105 mg sodium; Made with naturally sweetened yogurt: 285 calories, 8 g protein, 65 g carbohydrates, <1 g fat, trace saturated fat, 4 mg cholesterol, 6 g fiber, 119 mg sodium

chocolate peanut butter breakfast banana split

Hands-on Time: 4 MINUTES • *Hands-off Time:* NONE

Chocolate and peanut butter? Yes! Now we're talking. Not only will your kids be singing your praises when you throw together this breakfast in mere minutes, you'll be feeling like you're cheating with each decadent bite!

1/3 cup Fiber One or naturally sweetened fat-free vanilla yogurt
2 teaspoons chocolate syrup
1 small (6–7 inches) ripe banana, peeled
1 tablespoon all-natural creamy peanut butter
2 tablespoons low-fat granola without raisins

In a small bowl, mix the yogurt and chocolate syrup until swirled.

Cut the banana in half lengthwise. Open it and place it, insides facing up, in a small banana split dish or medium shallow bowl. Spread the peanut butter evenly over the insides of the banana. Spoon the yogurt over the middle two-thirds. Top the yogurt with the granola. Serve immediately.

Makes 1 serving. Made with Fiber One yogurt: 334 calories, 9 g protein, 58 g carbohydrates, 9 g fat, 2 g saturated fat, 3 mg cholesterol, 8 g fiber, 112 mg sodium; Made with naturally sweetened yogurt: 346 calories, 10 g protein, 58 g carbohydrates, 9 g fat, 2 g saturated fat, 3 mg cholesterol, 5 g fiber, 121 mg sodium

chocolate raspberry breakfast sundae

Hands-on Time: 3 MINUTES • *Hands-off Time:* NONE

The combination of chocolate and raspberries is considered decadent by pretty much everyone. Here's a decadent breakfast that will keep you fit, healthy, and happy with each bite.

6-ounce container artificially sweetened or
    naturally sweetened raspberry or vanilla
    yogurt
3 tablespoons low-fat granola without raisins
1/2 cup fresh raspberries
1 1/2 teaspoons chocolate syrup

Spoon the yogurt into a sundae dish or small, deep bowl. Sprinkle the granola evenly over top, followed by the raspberries. Drizzle the syrup evenly over the top. Serve immediately.

Makes 1 serving. Made with naturally sweetened yogurt: 258 calories, 9 g protein, 56 g carbohydrates, 1 g fat, trace saturated fat, 5 mg cholesterol, 6 g fiber, 162 mg sodium; Made with artificially sweetened yogurt: 218 calories, 8 g protein, 47 g carbohydrates, 1 g fat, trace saturated fat, 4 mg choleserol, 5 g fiber, 154 mg sodium

pineapple coconut breakfast
banana split

Hands-on Time: 4 MINUTES • *Hands-off Time:* NONE

I am a huge fan of anything colada—piña colada, strawberry colada, even mango colada. This dish is a healthier twist on a banana colada that's great for breakfast or any time of the day. For a real treat, tuck the kids into bed at night, and then try it with a small spike of rum.

1 small (6–7 inches) ripe banana, peeled
1/3 cup low-fat, artificially sweetened piña colada yogurt
1 1/2 tablespoons canned, drained crushed pineapple
2 tablespoons low-fat granola without raisins
1 tablespoon sweetened flake coconut

Cut the banana in half lengthwise. Place the halves side by side in a banana split dish or medium shallow bowl. Spoon the yogurt over the middle two-thirds of the banana. Top the yogurt with the crushed pineapple. Sprinkle the granola and then coconut over the top of the pineapple. Serve immediately.

Makes 1 serving. 218 calories, 5 g protein, 47 g carbohydrates, 2 g fat, 1 g saturated fat, 2 mg cholesterol, 4 g fiber, 86 mg sodium

orange chocolate parfait

Hands-on Time: 3 MINUTES • *Hands-off Time:* NONE

This simple breakfast is great to eat on the go. Just mix the Grape-Nuts and chocolate chips directly into the yogurt carton and take the whole thing with you. Cleanup's as easy as tossing the container!

6-ounce container low-fat, naturally sweetened or fat-free, artificially sweetened orange cream or orange yogurt

1½ tablespoons crunchy high-fiber, low-sugar cereal (I used Grape-Nuts)

1 teaspoon mini chocolate chips

Spoon the yogurt into a small, deep bowl and sprinkle the cereal and chocolate chips over the top. Stir to combine. Serve immediately.

Makes 1 serving. Made with naturally sweetened yogurt: 231 calories, 6 g protein, 45 g carbohydrates, 3 g fat, 2 g saturated fat, 10 mg cholesterol, 2 g fiber, 134 mg sodium; Made with artificially sweetened yogurt: 151 calories, 7 g protein, 28 g carbohydrates, 2 g fat, <1 g saturated fat, 4 mg cholesterol, 2 g fiber, 152 mg sodium

raspberry lemonade smoothie

Hands-on Time: 5 MINUTES • *Hands-off Time:* NONE

Juice bar smoothies have justifiably gotten a bad rap because they're often chock-full of added sugar and calories. This twist on traditional raspberry lemonade uses only 1 teaspoon of honey, and the rest of the sweetness comes from real fruit. Note that it's important to use frozen fruit in smoothies because if you use too many ice cubes to try to get that thick consistency, you'll end up with a watery, not-as-good-as-the-juice-bar's smoothie in minutes.

$^1\!/_2$ cup frozen raspberries

$^1\!/_2$ cup frozen mango cubes

$^1\!/_2$ cup fat-free artificially or naturally
sweetened lemon or lemon chiffon
yogurt

$^1\!/_4$ cup fresh lemon juice

1 teaspoon honey or more, to taste

4 medium ice cubes

Put the raspberries, mango, yogurt, lemon juice, 1 teaspoon honey, and the ice in the jar of a blender with ice-crushing ability. Make sure the lid is on tight. Using the purée or ice crush setting, blend the ingredients until they are relatively smooth, about 1 minute. Then blend on the liquefy or high speed setting for about 10 seconds, or until the mixture is completely smooth. Add additional honey, if desired. Serve immediately.

Makes 1 (12-ounce) smoothie. Made with artificially sweetened yogurt: 198 calories, 7 g protein, 47 g carbohydrates, <1 g fat, 0 g saturated fat, 3 mg cholesterol, 5 g fiber, 88 mg sodium; Made with naturally sweetened yogurt: 218 calories, 6 g protein, 52 g carbohydrates, <1 g fat, 0 g saturated fat, 3 mg cholesterol, 6 g fiber, 71 mg sodium

apple cinnamon (breakfast) bruschetta

Hands-on Time: 7 MINUTES, INCLUDING TIME TO MAKE THE TOPPING •
Hands-off Time: NONE

Toast the mini pita in a toaster or toaster oven. Just be careful, if using a toaster, when removing them. I keep a set of wooden chopsticks on hand for safely "fishing" smaller items from the toaster.

I love this dish following a quick breakfast omelet or scramble. It has only about 100 calories, so it provides a guilt-free sweet treat after lean protein to fill me (or you!) up.

If you're making this for small children, they're likely to love it even more if you mix the bruschetta topping with the yogurt and then stuff it in the pitas—they're apt to find it easier to eat.

2 tablespoons Fiber One or naturally
    sweetened fat-free vanilla yogurt
Pinch cinnamon
2 whole-wheat mini (3-inch-diameter) pita
    circles, toasted
6 tablespoons Apple Cinnamon Bruschetta
    Topping (recipe follows), divided

In a small bowl, mix the yogurt with the cinnamon.

Place the pita circles on a small plate. Top each pita evenly with half of the yogurt mixture and then half of the bruschetta topping. Serve immediately.

Makes 1 serving. Made with Fiber One yogurt: 102 calories, 4 g protein, 23 g carbohydrates, <1 g fat, 0 g saturated fat, 1 mg cholesterol, 5 g fiber, 146 mg sodium; Made with naturally sweetened yogurt: 106 calories, 4 g protein, 23 g carbohydrates, <1 g fat, 0 g saturated fat, <1 g cholesterol, 4 g fiber, 150 mg sodium

apple cinnamon bruschetta topping

Hands-on Time: 4 MINUTES • *Hands-off Time:* NONE

1 medium apple, cut into small cubes
(roughly ¼-inch)
2 teaspoons fresh lemon juice
½ teaspoon cinnamon

In a resealable plastic container, stir the apples, lemon juice, and cinnamon until well combined. Can be stored in the refrigerator for up to 2 days.

Makes 2 servings. Each (6-tablespoon) serving has: 43 calories, trace protein, 12 g carbohydrates, trace fat, 0 g saturated fat, 0 mg cholesterol, 3 g fiber, trace sodium

crunchy breakfast banana logs

Hands-on Time: 5 MINUTES • *Hands-off Time:* 15 MINUTES TO SET

Kids will definitely go for these logs. Make them for breakfast or even as an after-school snack. They're so delicious, the kids won't balk at eating fruit.

If you have them, feel free to use corn-on-the-cob holders to assist in coating the bananas. You don't absolutely need them, but they'll help keep the peanut butter where it belongs—on the bananas.

¼ cup crunchy high-fiber, low-sugar cereal
    (I used Grape-Nuts)
1 tablespoon all-natural creamy peanut butter
    (chunky won't work in this recipe)
1 small banana, peeled and cut into thirds
    crosswise

Pour the cereal into a medium shallow bowl.

Spoon the peanut butter into a small, shallow microwave-safe bowl. Microwave on medium until the peanut butter is just melted, 15 to 20 seconds.

Roll one piece of the banana in the peanut butter to lightly coat it on all sides. Transfer it to the cereal bowl and coat it evenly with the cereal. Place it in a medium resealable plastic container lined with parchment or waxed paper. Repeat with the remaining pieces and place them side by side in the container. Refrigerate them for at least 15 minutes. Serve chilled.

Makes 1 serving. 295 calories, 8 g protein, 50 g carbohydrates, 9 g fat, 1 g saturated fat, 0 mg cholesterol, 7 g fiber, 171 mg sodium

better burgers, sandwiches, & wraps

bacon cheeseburger

Hands-on Time: 8 MINUTES • *Hands-off Time:* TIME TO PREHEAT THE GRILL

Yes, a bacon cheeseburger. If you buy 96% lean beef and reduced-fat bacon pieces, you're good to go! Do note, if you're a fan of BBQ bacon cheeseburgers, just swap out the ketchup in this recipe for your favorite barbecue sauce. It will add about 10 calories but save you around 15 mg sodium.

    Look for the bacon pieces near the croutons and other salad ingredients in your favorite grocery store. Or, if you love them as much as I do, head to Costco and buy them in a big bag. Just store them in your refrigerator and you'll have them on hand to curb a bacon craving with less guilt.

4 ounces 96% lean ground beef

1 1/2 tablespoons 50% reduced-fat real bacon pieces (I used Hormel 50% Reduced-Fat Real Bacon Pieces)

1 teaspoon dried minced onion

Salt, to taste

1 (about 3 1/2-inch-diameter) whole-wheat or whole-grain hamburger bun

1/2 ounce light Swiss cheese slivers.

1 small leaf green lettuce

3 (1/4-inch-thick) slices plum tomato

1 tablespoon ketchup or barbecue sauce

Preheat a grill to high.

In a small bowl, mix the beef, bacon, and onion until well combined. Shape the beef into a patty about 1/2 inch larger in diameter than the bun. Lightly sprinkle both sides of the patty with salt. Grill the burger 1 to 2 minutes per side for medium-rare or until desired doneness is reached. (Do *not* smash the burger with a spatula.) Just before the burger is done, place the bun halves, insides face down, on a top grill rack or away from open flame to toast them. Add the cheese atop the patty to melt, 15 to 30 seconds.

Place the toasted bun bottom on a plate. Add the burger patty, the lettuce, and the tomato slices. Spread the ketchup or barbecue sauce over the inside of the bun top and flip it atop the burger. Serve immediately.

Makes 1 serving. 351 calories, 36 g protein, 29 g carbohydrates, 11 g fat, 4 g saturated fat, 80 mg cholesterol, 4 g fiber, 745 mg sodium

Bacon Cheeseburger with Powerhouse Polenta Fries (page 159)

saucy turkey chili burger

Hands-on Time: 8 MINUTES • *Hands-off Time:* TIME TO PREHEAT THE GRILL

Sure, if you pull into the drive-thru, chili burgers can be deadly. But here, using the leanest ground turkey with canned turkey chili, you can have a decadently drippy yet sensible meal that satisfies.

For another 60 calories and 2.5 grams of fat, you can even add an ounce of 75% light finely shredded Cheddar cheese.

3 tablespoons 98% or 99% fat-free canned turkey chili with beans
3 ounces 99% lean ground turkey
Salt and pepper, to taste
1 (about 3 1/2-inch-diameter) whole-wheat or whole-grain hamburger bun
Yellow mustard, to taste (optional)

Preheat a grill to high heat.

Spoon the chili into a small microwave-safe bowl and cover the bowl with a paper towel. (Alternatively, you can heat the chili in a small saucepan over medium heat.)

Line a flat work surface with waxed paper. With your hands, shape the turkey into a tight ball. Place it on the waxed paper and press it into a 4-inch-diameter patty. Season the patty with salt and pepper. Grill until it is no longer pink inside, about 2 minutes per side. During the last minute of cooking, if desired, toast the bun by placing it, insides face down, on a top grill rack or away from direct flame until just toasted.

Meanwhile, if microwaving the chili, microwave it on high in 30-second intervals, or until warmed through.

Place the bun bottom on a serving plate. Add the burger, then spoon the chili on top. If using, spread the mustard over the inside of the bun top. Add it to the burger. Serve immediately.

Makes 1 serving. 246 calories, 28 g protein, 28 g carbohydrates, 4 g fat, <1 g saturated fat, 39 mg cholesterol, 5 g fiber, 344 mg sodium

blue cheese portobello mushroom burger

Hands-on Time: 15 MINUTES • *Hands-off Time:* TIME TO PREHEAT THE GRILL

Looking for a tasty, healthy variation of a beef or turkey burger? Skip those processed veggie burgers and go for this all-natural alternative, the portobello. A portobello mushroom smothered with reduced-fat blue cheese crumbles is just as healthy as it is mouthwatering, and it is hearty enough to serve to even a meat lover.

1 teaspoon Worcestershire sauce

1/4 teaspoon extra virgin olive oil

Salt and pepper, to taste

1 medium portobello mushroom cap

3/4 ounce (about 3 tablespoons) crumbled reduced-fat blue cheese (I used Treasure Cave)

1 (about 3 1/2-inch-diameter) whole-wheat or whole-grain hamburger bun

1 small leaf green lettuce (any variety)

1 very thin slice of onion

2 teaspoons Dijon mustard (optional)

Preheat a grill to medium heat.

In a small, shallow bowl, using a fork, whisk the Worcestershire, olive oil, salt, and pepper until well combined.

Using a damp paper towel, clean the mushroom to remove any visible dirt. Then brush the Worcestershire mixture evenly over both sides. Grill it, beginning gills-side down, away from direct flame until tender, 3 to 5 minutes per side. During the last 2 minutes of cooking, top the gills evenly with the blue cheese to melt it, and toast the bun by placing the bun halves, insides face down, on a top grill rack or away from the flame for about 30 seconds.

Place the bun bottom on a small plate. Top it with the mushroom, followed by the lettuce, then the onion. Spread the inside of the bun top with mustard, if desired, and top the burger. Serve immediately.

Makes 1 serving. 224 calories, 12 g protein, 29 g carbohydrates, 7 g fat, 3 g saturated fat, 11 mg cholesterol, 5 g fiber, 562 mg sodium

drippin' kickin' burger

Buy preshaped burger patties to save time. If your favorite supermarket doesn't stock the 96% lean patties in the fresh meat case, check the freezer section; they're often found there. If you still can't find them, don't cheat—just shape the 96% lean beef yourself. You'll save about 30 calories and 4 grams of fat per 4-ounce burger over 93% lean meat and even more over buying a fattier ground beef.

2 tablespoons chili sauce (the one in the ketchup aisle, not near the Thai foods)

$1/8$ teaspoon hot pepper sauce, or more to taste

4-ounce 96% lean beef hamburger patty

Salt and pepper, to taste

$3/4$ ounce light Swiss cheese slivers

1 (about $3^{1}/2$-inch-diameter) whole-wheat or whole-grain hamburger bun

1 small leaf green lettuce

1 ($1/4$-inch-thick) large tomato slice, or a few smaller slices

1 very thin slice of onion

Preheat a grill to high heat.

In a small microwave-safe bowl, mix the chili sauce and hot pepper sauce.

Season both sides of the patty with salt and pepper. Grill it 1 to 2 minutes per side for medium-rare or until desired doneness is reached. During the last minute of cooking, add the cheese to the patty, and, if desired, toast the bun by placing it, insides face down, on a top grill rack or away from the flame until just toasted.

Meanwhile, microwave the chili sauce mixture on low for 15 to 30 seconds, or until just hot.

Place the bun bottom on a serving plate. Add the lettuce, tomato, and onion, followed by the burger. Spoon the sauce over the burger. Add the bun top. Serve immediately.

Makes 1 serving. 353 calories, 33 g protein, 34 g carbohydrates, 11 g fat, 4 g saturated fat, 70 mg cholesterol, 4 g fiber, 688 mg sodium

make you hot jalapeño burger

Hands-on Time: 9 MINUTES • *Hands-off Time:* TIME TO PREHEAT GRILL

One of the keys to making great extra-lean turkey burgers is to add moisture. Here, I quickly throw some egg substitute and bread crumbs into the turkey. Another key is the extra kick of flavor from the fresh jalapeños.

1 tablespoon egg substitute

1 tablespoon plain bread crumbs (whole wheat are great if you can find them)

4 ounces 99% lean ground turkey

Salt and pepper, to taste

Olive oil spray (from a spray bottle, not a store-bought, prefilled one that contains propellant; I used a Misto)

3/4 ounce very thinly sliced 75% light Cheddar cheese

1 (about 3 1/2-inch-diameter) whole-wheat or whole-grain hamburger bun

1 leaf green lettuce

1 thin, large tomato slice, or a few small slices

6 to 12 thin slices jalapeño chile

1 tablespoon low-fat mayonnaise (no more than 2 g fat per tablespoon; I used Best Foods/Hellmann's)

Preheat a grill to high heat.

In a small bowl, mix the egg substitute and bread crumbs. Mix in the turkey until the ingredients are well combined. Shape the turkey into a patty about 1/2 inch in diameter larger than the bun. Season with salt and pepper.

Lightly spray both sides of the patty with olive oil spray. Grill it until no longer pink inside, about 2 minutes per side. During the last minute of cooking, add the cheese to the patty. Also, if desired, toast the bun by placing it, insides face down, on a top grill rack or away from an open flame until just toasted, about 30 seconds.

Place the bun bottom on a serving plate. Add the lettuce, tomato, then jalapeño slices, followed by the patty. Spread the inside of the bun top evenly with the mayonnaise. Place the bun top on the burger and serve immediately.

Makes 1 serving. 333 calories, 41 g protein, 30 g carbohydrates, 7 g fat, 2 g saturated fat, 53 mg cholesterol, 4 g fiber, 635 mg sodium

buffalo blue cheese burger

Hands-on Time: 8 MINUTES • *Hands-off Time:* TIME TO PREHEAT GRILL

Traditional buffalo wings are fattening, but sometimes you still crave that buffalo flavor. Instead of over-indulging, opt for this burger to get those visions of dripping wing sauce and tangy blue cheese out of your head and into your tummy.

Look for preshaped patties (because they're also preweighed) to save time. This burger can be cooked in a grill pan or on a nonstick grill, but I love outdoor grilling when possible for optimum flavor without added fat.

1 teaspoon hot sauce, or more to taste (an all-natural one like Wing Time, not a thin one like Tabasco)

1 tablespoon low-fat mayonnaise (no more than 2 g fat per tablespoon; I used Best Foods/Hellmann's)

4 ounces 96% lean ground beef

$1/2$ ounce (2 tablespoons) reduced-fat blue cheese crumbles

1 (about $3^1/2$-inch-diameter) whole-grain or whole-wheat hamburger bun

1 small leaf green lettuce

3 ($1/4$-inch-thick) plum tomato slices

Preheat a grill to high heat.

In a small bowl, using a small whisk or a fork, stir the hot sauce and mayonnaise until well combined. Set aside.

In a second small bowl, mix the beef and the blue cheese until well combined. Shape the beef into a patty $1/2$ inch wider in diameter than the bun (about 4 inches).

Grill the patty 1 to 2 minutes per side for medium-rare, or until desired doneness is reached. (Do *not* smash the burger with a spatula.) Just before the burger is done cooking, place the bun halves, insides face down, on an upper grill rack or away from direct flame to toast, watching them carefully.

Place the bun bottom on a plate. Top with the burger patty, lettuce, then tomatoes. Spread the buffalo sauce mixture over the inside of the bun top and flip it atop the burger. Serve immediately.

Makes 1 serving. 322 calories, 30 g protein, 28 g carbohydrates, 11 g fat, 4 g saturated fat, 68 mg cholesterol, 5 g fiber, 609 mg sodium

ahi tuna steak sandwich

Hands-on Time: 8 MINUTES • *Hands-off Time:* NONE

It's important, when making this sandwich, that you have all of your ingredients prepped and ready to go before cooking the tuna—you don't want the tuna sitting after it's cooked.

When selecting tuna for this dish, be sure to get tuna that is undoubtedly sushi or sashimi grade. Cutting corners and using any fresh tuna is not an option on this one. Also, make sure the tuna is bright red all over. If the edges are just a bit murky or even the slightest shade of brown, don't buy it. If it's fresh, it will be bright red throughout.

1/4 teaspoon prepared wasabi or 2 teaspoons prepared horseradish, or to taste

2 tablespoons low-fat mayonnaise (no more than 2 g fat per tablespoon; I used Best Foods/Hellmann's)

1/2 teaspoon extra virgin olive oil

2 (4-ounce) sashimi- or sushi-grade ahi tuna fillets

Sea salt and freshly ground black pepper, to taste

2 (about 3 1/2-inch-diameter) whole-wheat or whole-grain hamburger buns

6 thin plum tomato slices, or 2 to 4 larger slices

1 small leaf green lettuce, cut in half, or more to taste

Stir the wasabi or horseradish into the mayonnaise until well combined. Add more to taste, if desired. Set aside.

If the fillets are thicker than 3/4 inch or are not at least slightly larger than the buns, place them between 2 sheets of waxed paper or plastic wrap. Using the flat side of a meat mallet or the bottom of a skillet, pound them until they are slightly larger than the buns.

Rub the olive oil evenly over the entire fillets. Season both sides of the fillets with salt and pepper.

Place a small nonstick skillet over high heat. When very hot (but not so hot that the pan smokes), add the fillets. Sear them so the outsides are golden brown in spots but the insides are rare, 30 seconds to 1 minute per side.

Meanwhile, place half a lettuce leaf and 3 tomato slices on each bun bottom. Top each with 1 fillet. Spoon half of the reserved mayonnaise mixture on each bun top and flip them atop the sandwiches. Serve immediately.

Makes 2 servings. Each (1-sandwich) serving has: 298 calories, 32 g protein, 27 g carbohydrates, 7 g fat, <1 g saturated fat, 0 mg cholesterol, 4 g fiber, 395 mg sodium

blackened salmon sandwich

Hands-on Time: 10 to 12 MINUTES • *Hands-off Time:* NONE

I use wild-caught salmon when possible because it's lower in fat than farm-raised. That said, it is more expensive and harder to find in many areas of the country, especially if you're buying it fresh. But you can always check the freezer section, where it is more commonly found. If you do end up using farm-raised salmon, add about 12 calories and 1.5 grams of fat per ounce over wild-caught.

1 (3$\frac{1}{2}$-ounce) salmon fillet, skin and bones removed (I used wild-caught)

Olive oil spray (from a spray bottle, not a store-bought, prefilled one that contains propellant; I used a Misto)

1 teaspoon Cajun or blackened seasoning (choose one where salt is not listed as the first ingredient)

1 (about 3$\frac{1}{2}$-inch-diameter) whole-grain or whole-wheat hamburger bun

$\frac{1}{4}$ cup arugula leaves or other green lettuce

2 ($\frac{1}{4}$-inch-thick) tomato slices

1 very thin slice of onion (I used red onion)

$\frac{1}{2}$ tablespoon honey mustard

Lightly mist both sides of the fillet with spray. Sprinkle the seasoning evenly over both sides.

Place a small nonstick skillet over medium-high heat. When the pan is hot, add the salmon. Cook the fillets 1 to 2 minutes per side, or until the outsides are just lightly browned. Then reduce the heat to medium and continue cooking until the fillet is pale pink throughout, 2 to 3 minutes per side.

Place the bun bottom on a serving plate. Top it with the salmon, followed by the arugula, tomato, then onion. Spread the mustard over the inside of the bun top. Flip it atop the sandwich. Serve immediately.

Makes 1 serving. 289 calories, 24 g protein, 28 g carbohydrates, 10 g fat, 1 g saturated fat, 55 mg cholesterol, 4 g fiber, 717 mg sodium

super-packed family-sized grilled chicken grinder

Hands-on Time: 8 MINUTES: • *Hands-off Time:* NONE

The key to this sandwich is perfectly cooked chicken. Because this sub is jam-packed with grilled chicken, it's important that the chicken isn't dry or the sandwich will be dry. Just follow the directions for Basic Grilled Chicken (page 219), and you'll be well on your way to prepping a delicious sub for the entire family. I love making the chicken on Sunday so I have it to use in recipes like this one over the next few days.

1 (8-ounce) whole-grain or whole-wheat baguette

1/4 cup low-fat mayonnaise (no more than 2 g fat per tablespoon; I used Best Foods/Hellman's)

1/2 cup shredded lettuce

1 large tomato, thinly sliced

1/2 cup onion slivers

1/2 cup red or green bell pepper strips

1 pound Basic Grilled Chicken (see page 219), breasts cut in half on the diagonal or to best fit, or lean, store-bought grilled chicken breasts or strips

Dried oregano, to taste

Crushed red pepper flakes, to taste

On a large cutting board, cut the baguette lengthwise as if you're cutting a single sandwich roll (be careful not to separate the halves). Spread the mayonnaise evenly over the inside of the bottom half of the baguette. Evenly add the lettuce, tomato, onion, and peppers, followed by the chicken (the sandwich will be very full). Sprinkle oregano and red pepper flakes evenly over it. Cut the sandwich crosswise into 4 equal pieces. Serve immediately.

Makes 4 servings. Each (1/4 sub, about 9 1/2 ounces) serving has: 312 calories, 32 g protein, 33 g carbohydrates, 5 g fat, <1 g saturated fat, 65 mg cholesterol, 3 g fiber, 440 mg sodium

mafia's favorite turkey sandwich

Hands-on Time: 5 MINUTES • *Hands-off Time:* NONE

Growing up on the East Coast, it wasn't hard to find all sorts of pickled peppers, both sweet and hot. You couldn't go anywhere near a cheesesteak place in Philly without seeing them. In Los Angeles, they're less common, but most grocery stores have at least one or two varieties. One of my favorites is sweet cherry pepper rings. They add plenty of flavor without any fat— you can't go wrong with that.

2 slices whole-wheat or whole-grain bread (about 70 calories or less per slice)

4 ounces thinly sliced or shaved extra-lean smoked deli turkey (lower-sodium if possible)

1 slice reduced-fat provolone cheese (I used Sargento)

½ leaf green lettuce, or to taste

2 thin tomato slices

⅓ cup drained sweet cherry pepper rings or strips (I used Mezzetta)

1 tablespoon low-fat mayonnaise (no more than 2 g fat per tablespoon; I used Best Foods/Hellmann's)

Place one slice of bread on a serving plate. Top it evenly with the turkey, followed by the cheese, lettuce, tomato, and peppers. Spread the mayonnaise evenly over the second slice of bread, then flip the slice atop the sandwich. Serve immediately.

Makes 1 serving. 324 calories, 35 g protein, 34 g carbohydrates, 7 g fat, 2 g saturated fat, 70 mg cholesterol, 5 g fiber, 1,629 mg sodium

chipotle turkey sandwich

Hands-on Time: 4 MINUTES: • *Hands-off Time:* NONE

I've found people—even those concerned about sodium—often turn to the good old turkey sandwich as if it's the perfect healthy lunch. This always amazes me, because 4 ounces of your typical deli turkey (as opposed to homemade) have about 1,330 mg sodium, while its lower-sodium counterpart (which rarely has great flavor) still has 680 mg sodium. Two slices of bread have about 320 mg, a 1-ounce slice of cheese has 140 mg, and light jarred mayonnaise has about 120 mg per tablespoon (mustard has 170 g per tablespoon). Add those together, and this otherwise healthy sandwich has over 2,080 mg sodium. If you're ordering it out, it could have even more.

Though I do believe the turkey sandwich has a place in our diets, this is must-know information.

1 tablespoon low-fat mayonnaise (no more than 2 g of fat per tablespoon; I used Best Foods/Hellmann's)

1/8 teaspoon chipotle chili pepper (found in the spice aisle in jars; I used McCormick)

2 slices whole-wheat or whole-grain bread (70 calories or less per slice)

4 ounces thinly sliced or shaved extra-lean salsa, Southwest, or similarly seasoned deli turkey (found at the deli counter)

1 slice reduced-fat Colby or Monterey Jack cheese (I used Sargento)

1/2 leaf green lettuce, or to taste

3 thin tomato slices, or more to taste

1 thin red onion slice, or more to taste

In a small bowl, mix together the mayonnaise and chipotle.

Place one slice of bread on a serving plate. Top it with the turkey followed by the cheese, lettuce, tomato, and onion. Spread the chipotle mayonnaise evenly over the second slice of bread, then top the sandwich. Serve immediately.

Makes 1 serving. 344 calories, 30 g protein, 42 g carbohydrates, 9 g fat, 4 g saturated fat, 60 mg cholesterol, 5 g fiber, 1,380 mg sodium.

turkey provolone toaster sandwich

Hands-on Time: 5 MINUTES •
Hands-off Time: TIME TO PREHEAT TOASTER OVEN PLUS 5 MINUTES

This sandwich is great as a snack. The recipe makes only a half-sandwich, but it's a meaty half-sandwich (great protein-to-carb ratio). I often eat it with an orange or banana, and it's the perfect amount of food.

Did you know that 4 ounces of deli turkey (or other deli meat) often contain as much as 1,200 mg sodium? If you're watching your sodium, oven-roast your own skinless turkey breast at home and slice it down very thinly for deli meat. This will not only save you money but also allow you to control the amount of salt in the meat. If you can't roast your own turkey breast, be sure to look for lower-sodium varieties of deli turkey.

1 slice rye bread, cut in half crosswise

4 ounces thinly sliced lean turkey breast or lean, lower-sodium deli turkey

1 slice reduced-fat provolone cheese (I used Sargento), cut in half

Preheat a toaster oven or the oven to 400°F.

Place one bread half-slice on a small baking sheet. Top it evenly with one of the cheese halves, the turkey, and then the remaining piece of cheese. Top that with the remaining half-slice of bread. Bake until the cheese is melted and the bread is lightly toasted, about 5 minutes. Serve immediately.

Makes 1 serving. 255 calories, 34 g protein, 15 g carbohydrates, 7 g fat, 2 g saturated fat, 52 mg cholesterol, 1 g fiber, 505 mg sodium

baked brie turkey wrap

Hands-on Time: 4 MINUTES (MICROWAVE) OR 4 TO 6 MINUTES (STOVETOP) •
Hands-off Time: NONE

To brie or not to brie . . . that is the quandary for many. Well, now that I've found ways to stave off the cravings without overindulging, I'm definitely a happy camper. Though the flavor is subtle here, the brie is great paired with the cranberry sauce and arugula leaves. In minutes, you'll feel like you're eating at a gourmet sandwich shop, but without the gourmet sandwich consequences.

1 (about 8-inch-diameter) reduced-fat, whole-wheat flour tortilla

1 ounce light brie, cut into slivers as thin as possible

1 tablespoon cranberry sauce (preferably jarred and all-natural rather than canned)

3½ ounces shaved, extra-lean roasted turkey (preferably lower-sodium)

¼ cup arugula leaves

Microwave Instructions

Place the tortilla on a microwave-safe dinner plate. Add the brie slivers side by side to cover as much as possible of a 3-inch-wide strip down the middle of the tortilla, starting at one edge and stretching to about 2 inches short of the opposite edge. Microwave on high for 10 to 20 seconds, or until the brie is slightly melted (do not overcook). Top the brie with the cranberry sauce, followed by the turkey and then the arugula leaves. Fold the bottom edge over the filling, and then fold in the sides to create an open-ended wrap.

Stovetop Instructions

Follow the microwave instructions, except instead of melting the brie in the microwave, place a medium nonstick skillet over medium heat. When hot, add the tortilla to the pan (no need to add any fat) and add the brie slivers side by side to cover as much as possible of a 3-inch-wide strip down the middle of the tortilla, starting at one edge and stretching to about 2 inches short of the opposite edge. Heat the tortilla and cheese for 4 to 5 minutes, or until the brie is slightly melted.

Makes 1 serving. 296 calories, 31 g protein, 32 g carbohydrates, 7 g fat, 3 g saturated fat, 51 mg cholesterol, 2 g fiber, 1,184 mg sodium

ready-to-run roast beef pocket

Hands-on Time: 5 MINUTES • *Hands-off Time:* NONE

If you're looking for a healthy lunch, look no further. This sandwich comes together in minutes, packs easily, and carries well. And if you use homemade roast beef (or a fresh, extra-lean cut roast from the grocery store), it's also not much higher in fat, but much lower in sodium than your typical turkey sandwich.

1 tablespoon low-fat mayonnaise (2 g fat or less per tablespoon; I used Best Foods/ Hellmann's)

1 teaspoon prepared horseradish

1 (6^1/2-inch) whole-wheat or whole-grain pita circle

^{1}/2 cup alfalfa sprouts

3 thin tomato slices

1 thin red onion slice, or more to taste

4 ounces thinly sliced or shaved Simple Grilled London Broil (see page 221), Easy-As-Can-Be Pot Roast (see page 109), or other extra-lean roast beef

In a small bowl, mix the mayonnaise and horseradish until well combined.

Cut off one-third of the pita circle and save it for another recipe (like for dipping with the Wow 'em White Bean Dip; see page 102). Spread the mayonnaise mixture evenly on one side of the inside of the pocket. Add the sprouts, tomato, and onion. Top the vegetables evenly with the roast beef. Serve immediately or wrap the pocket in plastic wrap for up to 8 hours and refrigerate it until ready to serve.

Makes 1 serving. 207 calories, 27 g protein, 18 g carbohydrates, 5 g fat, 2 g saturated fat, 49 mg cholesterol, 3 g fiber, 431 mg sodium

santa fe chicken melt with guacamole

Hands-on Time: 8 MINUTES • *Hands-off Time:* TIME TO PREHEAT THE BROILER

When using your broiler, pay close attention to the cooking time of whatever it is you're making. The cheese on the top of this sandwich can go from perfectly melted and bubbly to burned in just a few seconds. And keep in mind that oven settings vary, especially broiler heat. I found this sandwich was perfectly warmed and melted around 1 minute, but that time could definitely be different based on the intensity of your individual broiler.

1 slice whole-wheat or whole-grain bread (70 calories or less per slice), toasted

4 ounces Basic Grilled Chicken (see page 219), or lean, store-bought grilled chicken breast, cut into thin slivers

1 canned whole mild green chile

1 ($1/4$-inch-thick) slice beefsteak tomato, or 2 ($1/4$-inch-thick) smaller slices

1 ounce very thinly sliced 75% light Cheddar (I used Cabot's)

1 tablespoon prepared guacamole (2 g of fat or less per tablespoon)

Preheat the broiler. Line a small baking sheet with foil.

Place the bread on the baking sheet. Top it with the chicken slices, followed by the chile, then the tomato. Lay the cheese evenly over the top. Broil until the cheese is melted (be careful not to burn it) and the chicken is slightly warmed through, 45 seconds to 1 minute. Top with guacamole. Serve immediately.

Makes 1 serving. 297 calories, 38 g protein, 17 g carbohydrates, 8 g fat, 2 g saturated fat, 74 mg cholesterol, 3 g fiber, 508 mg sodium

fully loaded turkey burrito pocket

Hands-on Time: 10 to 15 MINUTES • *Hands-off Time:* NONE

Some fresh salsas or pico de gallos contain a lot of moisture. If your salsa or pico de gallo seems watery, drain it in a strainer to prevent the burrito from becoming soggy.

Though it will take a bit longer, you can use turkey filets and cut them into strips if your store doesn't carry the strips. Or, better yet, ask your butcher to cut the filets into strips for you so you don't spend any unnecessary time in the kitchen.

4 ounces packaged raw turkey breast strips

1/2 teaspoon salt-free Southwest or Mexican seasoning (I used Southwest Chipotle Mrs. Dash)

Olive oil spray

1 (about 8-inch-diameter) reduced-fat, whole-wheat flour tortilla

1 tablespoon light sour cream

3/4 ounce (about 1/4 cup plus 2 tablespoons) finely shredded 75% light Cheddar (I used Cabot's)

1/4 cup shredded lettuce

3 tablespoons well-drained fresh salsa or pico de gallo

In a small bowl, toss the turkey with the seasoning until well combined.

Place a medium nonstick skillet over medium-high heat. When it's hot, mist the pan with spray and add the turkey. Cook the strips, stirring occasionally, until lightly browned and no longer pink inside, 2 to 4 minutes. Remove the strips to a bowl and cover to keep warm.

Reduce the heat to medium. Place the tortilla in the pan (no need to add fat). Cook for 30 seconds to 1 minute per side, or until just warmed.

Place the tortilla on a serving plate. Spread the sour cream in a 3-inch-wide strip down the center, leaving the bottom 3 inches of the tortilla bare (so you can fold the bare tortilla up and over part of the filling). Top the sour cream with the cheese, lettuce, salsa, and then the turkey. Fold in the sides of the tortilla over the filling and then fold up the bottom. Serve immediately.

Makes 1 serving. 307 calories, 39 g protein, 28 g carbohydrates, 6 g fat, 2 g saturated fat, 58 mg cholesterol, 2 g fiber, 420 mg sodium

southwest chicken open-ended wrap

Hands-on Time: 4 MINUTES • *Hands-off Time:* NONE

Open-ended wraps are a great way to ensure a balanced meal. A recommended serving of protein is about 4 ounces per adult meal. To fully encase that much protein in a tortilla, you would have to use a tortilla that's higher in carbs than advised. So I keep many of my wraps partially open. That way I can stuff plenty of ingredients in them while keeping my meals in check. In this case, it's a balanced meal that happens to be brimming with fillings.

1 (about 8-inch-diameter) reduced-fat, whole-wheat flour tortilla

4 ounces store-bought Southwest-seasoned grilled chicken strips or pieces, or prepared Southwest Basic Grilled Chicken (see page 220)

Small handful of prewashed, chopped lettuce

2 tablespoons fresh salsa or pico de gallo, drained (refrigerated, not jarred, if at all possible)

1 tablespoon low-fat ranch dressing, plain or spicy Southwest flavor (I used Follow Your Heart)

Place the tortilla on a dinner plate. Top it with the chicken in a 3-inch-wide strip down the center of the tortilla, leaving 2 inches bare on one end. (So you can fold the bare tortilla up and over part of the filling.) Top the chicken with the lettuce, followed by the salsa. Drizzle the ranch dressing evenly over the top. Fold up the bare end of the tortilla over the filling, and then fold the sides of the tortilla over the middle. Serve immediately.

Makes 1 serving. 266 calories, 30 g protein, 26 g carbohydrates, 5 g fat, <1 g saturated fat, 65 mg cholesterol, 2 g fiber, 306 mg sodium

overstuffed chicken guacamole wrap

Hands-on: 5 MINUTES • *Hands-off Time:* NONE

This wrap is filled with plenty of fresh ingredients. To make it easier to handle, be sure to finely shred the lettuce and cut the chicken into cubes, as this really is an overstuffed wrap—after all, the drippier the better (and more decadent!), right?

1 (about 8-inch-diameter) reduced-fat, whole-wheat flour tortilla

2 tablespoons prepared guacamole (2 g of fat or less per tablespoon)

4 ounces Basic Grilled Chicken (see page 219) or lean store-bought chicken breast, cut into cubes

1/2 cup finely shredded green lettuce leaves (I used romaine)

1/4 cup finely chopped tomato

Place the tortilla on a serving plate. Starting at one edge, spread a 3-inch-wide strip of the guacamole down the center, leaving about 1 inch bare at the opposite edge. (So you can fold the bare tortilla up and over part of the filling.) Place the chicken, lettuce, and tomato evenly on top of the guacamole. Fold up the bare edge of the tortilla, and then roll the sides over the filling to make an open wrap. Serve immediately, or wrap in plastic wrap and refrigerate for up to 6 hours.

Makes 1 serving. Each serving has: 306 calories, 31 g protein, 28 g carbohydrate, 9 g fat, 1 g saturated fat, 65 mg cholesterol, 5 g fiber, 287 mg sodium

open-ended BBQ chicken wrap

Hands-on Time: 4 MINUTES • *Hands-off Time:* NONE

This wrap is a quick and easy twist on one of my favorite pizzas. I love the combination of barbecue sauce and goat cheese dripping from meaty bites of fresh chicken with a kick of fresh cilantro. Yum! I think you will too.

4 ounces Basic Grilled Chicken (see page 219) or lean store-bought grilled chicken, thinly sliced

1 tablespoon plus 1 teaspoon barbecue sauce (look for one with 9 g of sugar or less per tablespoon)

1 (about 8-inch-diameter) reduced-fat whole-wheat flour tortilla

1/2 ounce (2 tablespoons) goat cheese crumbles

A few baby spinach leaves

A few red onion slivers

1 tablespoon chopped fresh cilantro leaves

In a small bowl, mix the chicken and barbecue sauce.

Place the tortilla on a dinner plate. Spread the cheese in an even 3-inch-wide strip down the center of the tortilla, leaving 2 inches bare on one end. (So you can fold the bare tortilla up and over part of the filling.) Top with the chicken, spinach, red onion, and cilantro. Fold up the bare end of the tortilla over the filling, and then fold the sides of the tortilla over the middle. Serve immediately.

Makes 1 serving. 321 calories, 32 g protein, 33 g carbohydrates, 8 g fat, 3 g saturated fat, 72 mg cholesterol, 2 g fiber, 527 mg sodium

amazing appetizers & savory snacks

enchizza

Hands-on Time: 8 MINUTES •
Hands-off Time: TIME TO PREHEAT OVEN PLUS 10 to 14 MINUTES

This dish is a simple marriage of an enchilada and pizza that has become a favorite of mine. If you're craving enchiladas, this is a great shortcut, because it doesn't involve laboring over a big pot of sauce or the time-consuming process of rolling enchiladas. Canned enchilada sauce is a great ingredient to have on hand because it's generally low-fat and has great flavor, and it can be used for more recipes than just enchiladas, like my Mexican Cocktail Meatballs (see page 107).

1 (about 6-inch-diameter) yellow or white corn tortilla

4 ounces Basic Grilled Chicken (see page 219) or lean, store-bought grilled chicken, sliced into bite-sized strips or pieces

3 tablespoons medium red chili enchilada sauce, divided

1 ounce (about 1/2 cup) finely shredded 75% light Cheddar cheese (I used Cabot's)

1 tablespoon canned sliced black olives

Preheat the oven to 400°F.

Bake the tortilla on a small nonstick baking sheet for 5 to 7 minutes per side, or until it is completely crisp. If air bubbles form while cooking, poke them with a fork, and then use a spatula or oven mitt to carefully press the air out. Remove the sheet from the oven.

Meanwhile, in a medium bowl, gently toss the chicken with 2 tablespoons of the enchilada sauce until it's well coated.

Place the chicken mixture on the tortilla, leaving 1/2 inch all around the edge bare. Sprinkle the cheese evenly over the top of the chicken, followed by the olives.

Transfer the sheet to the oven and bake the pizza for 2 to 4 minutes, or until the cheese is completely melted. Drizzle the remaining 1 tablespoon enchilada sauce evenly over the top of the pizza. Let it stand for 3 minutes, then slice into 4 equal wedges. Serve immediately.

Makes 1 serving. 279 calories, 37 g protein, 15 g carbohydrates, 7 g fat, 2 g saturated fat, 75 mg cholesterol, 2 g fiber, 556 mg sodium

grilled chicken & caramelized onion flatbread with blue cheese

Hands-on Time: 5 MINUTES (ONIONS MUST BE MADE IN ADVANCE) •
Hands-off Time: TIME TO PREHEAT GRILL PLUS 3 TO 5 MINUTES
TO GRILL PLUS 5 MINUTES TO STAND

When I was a child, we went to Chuck E. Cheese's for our birthdays. In addition to all of the cool games and the characters, I loved that they cut their pizzas into squares instead of wedges. Not only could you get more crust or less crust as you like (I'm a less-crust girl), I got to eat a number of pieces, since they're petite. Here, I've cut the flatbread into squares to distinguish it from other pizzas . . . and because it just feels more decadent.

If you're making this pizza on a charcoal grill, heat the coals until they are hot and covered with gray ash. Then place the pizza on the grill about 5 inches from the coals for best results. Cover and grill for 3 to 4 minutes.

1 (10-ounce) Boboli whole-wheat pizza crust

Olive oil spray (from a spray bottle, not a store-bought, prefilled one that contains propellant; I used a Misto)

8 ounces Basic Grilled Chicken (see page 219) or lean store-bought grilled chicken breast, cut into 1/2-inch pieces

1 recipe Easier-Than-Caramelized Onions (see page 225)

1 teaspoon dried rosemary

1 1/2 ounces (about 1/3 cup) reduced-fat blue cheese crumbles

Preheat a grill to medium heat. Lightly mist the bottom of the crust with spray. Place the crust on a metal pizza peel or cookie sheet without a lip.

Top the crust evenly with the chicken, then the onions, rosemary, and blue cheese.

Carefully slide the pizza onto the grill. Grill it until the cheese melts and the dough is crisped but not burned, 3 to 5 minutes. Carefully slide it back onto the peel or sheet (you may want to use tongs to drag it on) and let it stand 5 minutes. Slice the pizza into 16 squares and serve immediately.

NOTE: Nutrition information is based on 2 average-sized slices; corner pieces are smaller.

Makes 8 servings. Each (2-piece) serving (see Note) has: 160 calories, 12 g protein, 19 g carbohydrates, 5 g fat, 2 g saturated fat, 19 mg cholesterol, 3 g fiber, 278 mg sodium

pigs in comforters

Every New Year's Eve when I was a kid, we had pigs in blankets, chips with dip (see my makeover, Fixed-Up French Onion Dip, on page 100), and mini-pizzas. And that was pretty much the only time we ever had them, so I have such warm, celebratory memories associated with these foods.

The very first time I was on Good Morning America, it was on New Year's Eve and I was showing America how to throw together a last-minute, healthy New Year's Eve party. I made bite-sized pigs in blankets. Here, I've sped up the preparation time so you can eat this favorite in minutes any time of the year.

Be sure to buy biscuits with only 1.5 grams of fat or less per 2-biscuit serving. I've found that many private labels make them (so be sure to check those), as does Pillsbury.

Olive oil spray

5 low-fat beef hot dogs (I used Hebrew National)

1 can (10-count) refrigerated buttermilk or home-style biscuit dough (1.5 g of fat or less per 2-biscuit serving)

5 tablespoons mustard, optional

Prehead the oven to 375°F. Place a sheet of parchment over a medium baking sheet. Lightly mist it with spray.

Using 2 biscuits side by side, wrap each hot dog so only about 1 inch of the hot dog is exposed at each end. Roll the wrapped hot dogs back and forth on the cutting board to tightly seal the seams. Place the dogs at least $1/4$ inch apart, seams down, on the prepared baking sheet. Bake them until the dough is lightly browned and the dogs are hot, 13 to 15 minutes. Serve immediately with your favorite mustard for dipping, if desired.

Makes 5 pigs. Each pig has: 145 calories, 9 g protein, 23 g carbohydrates, 3 g fat, 1 g saturated fat, 15 mg cholesterol, 1 g fiber, 760 mg sodium

silly easy stromboli bites

Hands-on Time: 5 MINUTES •
Hands-off Time: TIME TO PREHEAT OVEN PLUS 12 TO 15 MINUTES

Having been raised on the East Coast, I thought everyone knew what stromboli is—you really couldn't go into a casual Italian restaurant without seeing it on the menu. Plus, my mother made it often. When I moved to the West Coast, I found most people had no idea what stromboli is. In case you aren't familiar with it, stromboli is traditionally made by taking bread dough, flattening it into a rectangle, layering it with Italian ingredients (my family's favorite was pepperoni and provolone), and then rolling it, jelly roll style. You seal the ends and bake it, so it's like a stuffed loaf when it emerges from the oven. When we served it at cocktail parties, we would always cut it into slices and serve the pieces on their sides so they looked like pinwheels.

This recipe is a much less fattening version of this Italian favorite. It is still a treat, but you won't need to spend hours and hours on a treadmill after you eat it.

1 (about 8-inch-diameter) reduced-fat, whole-wheat flour tortilla

1¼ ounces (¼ cup plus 2½ tablespoons) finely shredded low-fat mozzarella cheese (no more than 2.5 g of fat per ounce; I used Lucerne, found at Safeway chains)

12 slices turkey pepperoni

2 tablespoons low-fat marinara sauce (lower-sodium if possible), reheated if necessary

Preheat the oven to 400°F.

Place the tortilla on a cutting board or flat surface. Sprinkle the cheese evenly over the tortilla. Place the pepperoni evenly over the cheese.

Tuck in the opposite sides of the tortilla, as you would with a burrito, and then roll it as tightly as possible, creating a log. Wrap the log in foil. Place it directly on an oven rack and bake it until the cheese is completely melted, 12 to 15 minutes. Slice the stromboli into 6 slices, crosswise, and transfer the slices to a plate facing upward, so they look like pinwheels. Serve immediately, with marinara sauce for dipping.

Makes 1 serving. 242 calories, 19 g protein, 27 g carbohydrates, 8 g fat, 2 g saturated fat, 41 mg cholesterol, 3 g fiber, 922 mg sodium

scoopy joes

Hands-on Time: 8 MINUTES • *Hands-off Time:* NONE

We've all heard of sloppy joes. Well, now there's a new dish on the block. Instead of serving your favorite sloppy joes on a regular old hamburger bun, have some fun (and some crunch) with them by using Tostitos Baked! Scoops. If it's easier, feel free to sub in any baked tortilla chips for the scoops. They obviously won't look the same, but they'll taste just as great.

These joes can also be made with extra-lean ground turkey, but you'll need to add extra sauce because turkey is drier than beef. Using turkey in this recipe will save you about 3 grams of fat, but keep in mind that the extra sauce will add 95 mg of sodium per tablespoon.

4 ounces 96% lean ground beef
1/4 cup sloppy joe sauce (I used Manwich)
10 Tostitos Baked! Scoops

Place a small nonstick skillet over medium-high heat. When hot, add the beef. Using a spatula or wooden spoon, break the beef into bite-sized chunks, stirring as you do, until it is no longer pink, 2 to 3 minutes. Turn the heat to low and add the sauce until it is warmed through, 1 to 2 minutes. Serve immediately with the scoops for dipping (or fill the scoops for a fun appetizer, though that will take an extra couple of minutes).

Makes 1 serving. 242 calories, 24 g protein, 21 g carbohydrates, 7 g fat, 2 g saturated fat, 60 mg cholesterol, 2 g fiber, 545 mg sodium

pepperoni pizzadilla

Hands-on Time: 9 MINUTES • *Hands-off Time:* NONE

Who doesn't love pepperoni pizza? This recipe is a quicker, healthier alternative to the ordinarily fat-filled pie. It's also simple enough for kids to take part!

1 (about 8-inch-diameter) reduced-fat, whole-wheat flour tortilla (do not use a reduced-carb one)

1½ ounces (scant ½ cup) finely shredded reduced-fat mozzarella cheese (no more than 3 g fat per ounce; I used Lucerne, found at Safeway chains)

6 slices turkey pepperoni

1 tablespoon canned, drained, sliced black olives

2 pinches dried oregano

2 tablespoons low-fat marinara or pizza sauce (lower-sodium if possible), reheated if necessary

Place a medium nonstick skillet over medium heat. When hot, put the tortilla in the pan (no need to add any fat). Sprinkle half the cheese evenly over half the tortilla, followed by the pepperoni, the olives, the oregano, and the remaining cheese. Fold the bare half over the filling. Cook the tortilla until the cheese on the bottom half is mostly melted and the tortilla is lightly browned in spots, about 2 minutes. Then, using a spatula, carefully flip the quesadilla. Continue cooking it until the cheese is completely melted and the bottom is lightly browned in spots.

Slice the quesadilla into 4 wedges. Serve immediately with marinara on the side for dipping.

Makes 1 serving. 241 calories, 17 g protein, 28 g carbohydrates, 8 g fat, 2 g saturated fat, 29 mg cholesterol, 4 g fiber, 820 mg sodium

rock & roll pizza roll

Hands-on Time: 4 MINUTES •
Hands-off Time: TIME TO PREHEAT OVEN PLUS 12 to 15 MINUTES PLUS
2 MINUTES TO REST

You really can't beat this ridiculously easy and much healthier version of the pizza rolls you might find in your grocer's freezer. It's just as gooey, and it's guilt-free for you . . . and the kids. In fact, it can even be made with all-natural ingredients.

1 (about 8-inch-diameter) reduced-fat, whole-wheat flour tortilla (do not use a reduced-carb one)
2 tablespoons low-fat marinara or pizza sauce (lower-sodium, if possible)
1 (21 g) light string cheese (I used Sargento)

Preheat the oven to 400°F. Line a small baking sheet or dish with parchment.

Place the tortilla on a cutting board or flat work surface. Spread the marinara sauce to the edges of the tortilla.

Place the string cheese across one edge of the tortilla. Tuck in the sides of the tortilla over the cheese, and then roll it tightly, creating a log. Place the log on the prepared baking sheet and bake it until the cheese is completely melted, 12 to 15 minutes. Allow to cool for 2 minutes. Serve immediately.

Makes 1 serving. 174 calories, 10 g protein, 27 g carbohydrates, 5 g fat, 2 g saturated fat, 10 mg cholesterol, 3 g fiber, 400 mg sodium

thin & crispy margarita pizza

Hands-on Time: 12 MINUTES •
Hands-off Time: TIME TO PREHEAT OVEN PLUS 5 MINUTES TO REST

When I first saw the "herbs in tubes," as I call them, referring to Gourmet Garden's herb blends, I thought I wouldn't like them. But with one try, I became hooked, particularly to the garlic blend. This rendition of a margarita pizza is one of my favorite applications for them. It's insanely easy to throw together and especially tasty, considering the little amount of time it takes.

If you're having trouble finding these herbs, visit gourmetgarden.com and check out their store locator. Or you can look for herbs frozen in trays. At my local Trader Joe's, they sell frozen chopped garlic and chopped basil in trays from a brand called Dorot. Just be sure to measure the herbs yourself instead of relying on the measurements listed on the package (I found 1 teaspoon of basil was more than 1 cube, though the package says that 1 cube is equivalent to 1 teaspoon).

1 (about 8-inch-diameter) reduced-fat, whole-wheat flour tortilla (do not use a reduced-carb one)

1/2 teaspoon Gourmet Garden Garlic Blend or frozen herbs in trays (look for Gourmet Garden in tubes in the produce section or for frozen herbs at Trader Joe's)

1 1/2 teaspoons Gourmet Garden Basil Herb Blend or frozen herbs in trays (look for Gourmet Garden in tubes in the produce section or for frozen herbs at Trader Joe's)

1 1/2 ounces (scant 1/2 cup) finely shredded reduced-fat mozzarella cheese (no more than 2.5 g of fat per ounce; I used Lucerne, found at Safeway chains)

5 (1/4-inch-thick) plum tomato slices

Preheat the oven to 400°F.

Bake the tortilla on a small nonstick baking sheet for 3 to 4 minutes per side, or until it is completely crisp. If air bubbles form while cooking, poke them with a fork, and then use a spatula or oven mitt to carefully press the air out. Remove the sheet from the oven. Spread the garlic and basil evenly over all but the outer 1/2 inch of the tortilla. Top that evenly with the cheese and then the tomato slices.

Bake the pizza for 2 to 4 minutes, or until the cheese is completely melted. Allow it to cool for 5 minutes, and then slice it into 4 wedges. Serve immediately.

Makes 1 serving. 237 calories, 14 g protein, 31 g carbohydrates, 6 g fat, 2 g saturated fat, 15 mg cholesterol, 4 g fiber, 733 mg sodium

boneless honey BBQ "wings"

Hands-on Time: 10 TO 12 MINUTES • *Hands-off Time:* 5 MINUTES TO REST

When making these "wings," be sure your pan is piping hot and the chicken isn't overcrowded. The tenders should brown on the outside, and there should be no liquid in the pan as they cook to yield optimum—that is, decadent—results.

¼ cup barbecue sauce (find one with no more than 9 g of sugar and <1 g fat per tablespoon serving, preferably all-natural; I used OrganicVille)

2 tablespoons honey

¼ teaspoon garlic powder

Salt and pepper, to taste

16 chicken tenderloins (about 1 pound), trimmed

Olive oil spray

Combine the barbecue sauce and honey in a small bowl. Set aside.

Sprinkle the garlic powder, salt, and pepper over the tenderloins and toss them to combine.

Place a large nonstick skillet over high heat. When hot, lightly mist the skillet with spray and add the chicken strips side by side in a single layer (work in batches, if necessary—the chicken should sizzle when it hits the pan, or it's not hot enough). Cook the strips until they are lightly browned on the outside and no longer pink inside, 2 to 3 minutes per side. Turn the heat to low and return all wings to the pan, if working in batches. Pour the reserved barbecue sauce mixture over them and gently stir until they are well coated and the sauce is warm. Remove the pan from the heat. Let the wings sit in the pan for 5 minutes, and then toss them again (the sauce will stick better after sitting). Serve immediately.

Makes 4 servings. Each (4-wing) serving has: 164 calories, 26 g protein, 15 g carbohydrates, <1 g fat, 0 g saturated fat, 67 mg cholesterol, trace fiber, 244 mg sodium

asparagus roast beef roll-ups

Hands-on Time: 9 MINUTES (STOVETOP) OR 7 MINUTES (MICROWAVE) •
Hands-off Time: TIME TO BOIL WATER (STOVETOP) OR NONE (MICROWAVE)

This recipe is a great one to impress guests at your next cocktail party (though you'll have to multiply it). It's really quick and simple, yet it looks very decadent and time-consuming.

To make the roll-ups extra elegant for entertaining, wrap the roast beef close to the bottom of the spears, then stand them on a platter as pictured.

12 medium asparagus spears, trimmed by snapping off the ends where they break naturally
1 teaspoon prepared horseradish, or more to taste
2 tablespoons light sour cream
Salt and pepper, to taste
6 ounces thinly sliced or shaved Simple Grilled London Broil (page 221), Pot Roast (page 109), or extra-lean deli roast beef

Stovetop Instructions
Half-fill a large bowl with ice water.

Place a steamer rack insert in a large pot. Fill the pot with water so it reaches just below the steamer rack. Place the pot over high heat, cover it with a lid, and bring the water to a boil. Add the asparagus, cover the pot (leaving the lid slightly ajar), and steam the asparagus until crisp-tender, 3 to 5 minutes, depending on thickness. Transfer the asparagus to the bowl of ice water to stop the cooking. Drain well.

Meanwhile, in a small bowl, mix the horseradish and sour cream until well combined. Season with salt and pepper.

Lay $1^1/2$ ounces of the beef on a flat work surface or cutting board. Spread one-quarter (about $1/2$ tablespoon) of the horseradish mixture over the beef, leaving a small border. Place 3 asparagus spears at one of the narrower ends of each beef slice so the tips hang over. Roll the beef around the bundle of asparagus until you reach the other end of the beef. Repeat with the remaining roast beef, horseradish mixture, and asparagus to create 3 more roll-ups. Serve immediately.

Microwave Instructions
Follow the directions above, except instead of steaming the asparagus, add 1 tablespoon of water and the asparagus to a medium microwave-safe bowl or dish. Cover the dish with a microwave-safe plate. Microwave on high for 1 to 2 minutes, or until the asparagus is crisp-tender. Transfer the asparagus to a bowl of ice water to stop the cooking. Drain well.

Makes 2 servings. Each (2-bundle) serving has: 127 calories, 21 g protein, 5 g carbohydrates, 4 g fat, 2 g saturated fat, 42 mg cholesterol, 2 g fiber, 145 mg sodium

cukes in a blanket

It can be a bit tricky to spread the cheese over the cucumber because the cucumber pieces are so moist. But this super-simple snack is more than worth the mini-challenge!

1/3 English cucumber

2 (3/4-ounce) Light Original Swiss Laughing Cow cheese wedges

4 ounces thinly sliced or shaved extra-lean smoked deli turkey, preferably lower-sodium

Cut the cucumber in half lengthwise. Cut each half in half lengthwise, creating 4 spears or wedges. Then spread half of one cheese wedge over one of the cut sides of one cucumber spear. Lay 1 ounce of turkey slices on a flat surface. Place a cucumber wedge at one end of the turkey. Roll the cucumber in the turkey to create a log. Repeat with the remaining cucumbers, cheese, and turkey. Serve immediately.

Makes 2 servings. Each (2-wedge) serving has: 90 calories, 15 g protein, 2 g carbohydrates, 2 g fat, 1 g saturated fat, 40 mg cholesterol, <1 g fiber, 620 mg sodium

tuna sashimi with jalapeño

Hands-on Time: 4 MINUTES • *Hands-off Time:* NONE

One of my all-time favorite dishes to order at sushi bars is albacore or yellowtail sashimi with ponzu—a citrus-based soy sauce—and jalapeño (though they sometimes add way too much sesame oil for my taste). The name changes from menu to menu, but no matter the title, I absolutely love it. Here's an at-home version that's a cinch to throw together and super-nutritious. It's perfect for you or to impress your sushi-loving guests.

Though you might be tempted to omit the salt, I wouldn't recommend it. This is actually a great dish for exotic sea salt. A light sprinkle can add real depth to the dish.

4 ounces sashimi- or sushi-grade ahi tuna, cut into 8 equal slices

8 very thin jalapeño slices (rounds)

2 teaspoons ponzu sauce (look for it in the international section next to the soy sauce)

Sea salt, to taste

Arrange the tuna slices on a plate so the slices are touching in the center and point outward (like a starburst pattern). Place a piece of jalapeño in the center of each tuna slice. Drizzle the ponzu evenly over the top. Season with salt. Serve immediately.

Makes 1 serving. 153 calories, 28 g protein, 2 g carbohydrates, 3 g fat, 0 g saturated fat, 0 mg cholesterol, trace fiber, 282 mg sodium

"spicy tuna" salad

Hands-on Time: 3 MINUTES • *Hands-off Time:* NONE

This is a great spicy, low-carb snack when served with vegetables such as celery sticks and endive. It's also great served with baked tortilla chips or low-fat whole-grain crackers.

Until recently, canned tuna was most commonly available in 6-ounce cans. But lately, a lot of products have decreased in size—from cereals to ice cream to peanut butter, which now often has a bubble in the bottom of the jar to make it look as big as it once was—even though the prices have not gone down. Be wary of this when you determine how many calories you're consuming. The numbers on this dish are based on the 5-ounce can, not a 6-ounce one—which, by the way, generally contains only 3 1/2 ounces of tuna (the rest is liquid).

1 (5-ounce) can chunk light tuna in water, drained

1 tablespoon low-fat mayonnaise (no more than 2 g of fat per tablespoon; I used Best Foods/Hellmann's)

1/2 teaspoon chili garlic sauce, or more to taste

In a medium bowl, mix the tuna, mayonnaise, and chili garlic sauce until well combined. Season with additional chili garlic sauce, if desired. Serve immediately.

Makes 2 servings. Each (scant 1/4-cup) serving has: 65 calories, 13 g protein, 1 g carbohydrates, 1 g fat, trace saturated fat, 15 mg cholesterol, 0 g fiber, 268 mg sodium

hummus tuna bagels

Hands-on Time: 4 MINUTES • *Hands-off Time:* NONE

I worked on a teen weight-loss show by the producers of The Biggest Loser *that took place at a camp in Wisconsin. The night I arrived, I was talking to one of the producers about food, of course. He mentioned his ex-wife used to make tuna with hummus instead of mayo and serve it on bagels. He said that she suggested it to a restaurant and they started serving it. When I told him I was going to borrow the idea he said I had to credit his ex-wife—only he never mentioned her name. Though I created this myself, Matt's ex-wife deserves the credit for the general concept . . . whoever and wherever she is.*

1 (5-ounce) can chunk light tuna in water, drained

2 tablespoons garlic-flavored hummus (no more than 1.5 g of fat per tablespoon)

2 whole-wheat mini bagels, halved and toasted (I used Thomas')

4 very thin slices of red onion

In a small bowl, mix the tuna and hummus until well combined. Divide the tuna mixture evenly among the 4 bagel halves. Top each with 1 red onion slice. Serve immediately.

Makes 2 servings. Each (1 bagel; 2 halves) serving has: 200 calories, 18 g protein, 27 g carbohydrates, 3 g fat, trace saturated fat, 15 mg cholesterol, 4 g fiber, 428 mg sodium

garlic cheese breadsticks

Hands-on Time: 5 MINUTES • *Hands-off Time:* 18 TO 20 MINUTES

16 ounces store-bought, whole-wheat pizza dough, fresh or frozen, defrosted (I used Trader Joe's)

Olive oil spray

3 teaspoons garlic powder, plus more to taste, optional, divided

3 teaspoons reduced-fat grated Parmesan cheese, divided (look for it in a plastic canister or jar, not in the refrigerated section)

1 tablespoon light butter, melted

1 tablespoon chopped fresh parsley leaves

1/3 cup low-fat marinara or pizza sauce, preferably lower-sodium, reheated if necessary, optional

Preheat the oven to 350°F.

Press the dough evenly into a 9 × 9-inch non-stick baking pan or dish. Gently, being careful to keep the shape of the dough, lift the dough out of the pan onto a clean flat work surface. Lightly mist the pan with spray. Sprinkle 1 teaspoon of the garlic powder and 1 teaspoon of the Parmesan evenly over the bottom of the pan.

Lift the dough back into the pan (you may have to reshape it slightly). Sprinkle the remaining 2 teaspoons of garlic powder and Parmesan evenly over the dough. Using a dough scraper or butter knife, and without slicing all the way through the dough, cut the dough in half in one direction, then slice it into 8 equal pieces in the other to create 16 equal breadsticks. Bake the dough until golden brown and cooked through, 18 to 20 minutes.

Brush the butter evenly over the dough, then sprinkle the parsley evenly over that. Season with additional garlic powder, if desired. Serve immediately with marinara for dipping, if desired.

Makes 8 servings. Each (2-breadstick) serving has: 143 calories, 4 g protein, 25 g carbohydrates, 2 g fat, trace saturated fat, 2 mg cholesterol, 3 g fiber, 265 mg sodium

buff-corn

Looking for ways to cut more fat? The Biggest Loser *contestants have been known to swear by* I Can't Believe It's Not Butter! *spray instead of light butter when eating popcorn. As long as you don't add too much fat and too many calories, popcorn is a great snack. It's high in fiber and low in calories. You can eat a decent volume without eating too many calories.*

2 tablespoons yellow or white popcorn kernels

1/2 tablespoon light butter (stick, not tub; I used Challenge Light)

1 1/2 teaspoons hot sauce (a thick one like Wing Time, not a thin one like Tabasco), preferably all-natural

Pop the popcorn in an air popper or in the microwave using a microwave popping bowl according to package directions.

Meanwhile, add the butter and hot sauce to a small microwave-safe bowl. When the popping corn is popped, microwave the butter and sauce on high until the butter is mostly melted, 10 to 20 seconds. Stir it (it should then be melted).

Transfer the popped corn to a large serving bowl. Drizzle half of the butter mixture over the popcorn. Toss well, then drizzle the remaining butter mixture over the top. Toss again and serve immediately.

Makes 1 (2¾-cup) serving. 110 calories, 3 g protein, 17 g carbohydrates, 4 g fat, 2 g saturated fat, 8 mg cholesterol, 4 g fiber, 348 mg sodium

parmesan garlic soft pretzel

Hands-on Time: 3 MINUTES •
Hands-off Time: TIME TO PREHEAT OVEN PLUS 5 TO 6 MINUTES

Instead of succumbing to temptation at the mall, satisfy your craving for this savory pretzel at home with a fraction of the fat and calories. You'll definitely be glad you did when you save plenty of guilt and a lot of cash.

You can cook this pretzel in the microwave, but I think it's much more enjoyable (and no more calories) when it's cooked in the oven.

1 (64 g) frozen soft pretzel (1 g of fat or less per pretzel; I used Super Pretzel)

1/8 teaspoon garlic powder

1/2 teaspoon reduced-fat, grated Parmesan cheese (look for it in a plastic canister or jar, not in the refrigerated section)

1/2 teaspoon light butter, melted (stick, not tub; I used Challenge Light)

Bake the pretzel according to package directions (oven cooking is recommended), omitting any salt.

Meanwhile, in a small bowl, stir the garlic powder and Parmesan until well combined.

Brush the cooked pretzel evenly with the melted butter. Sprinkle the Parmesan mixture evenly over the top of the pretzel. Serve immediately.

Makes 1 serving. 175 calories, 5 g protein, 35 g carbohydrates, 2 g fat, trace saturated fat, 4 mg cholesterol, 1 g fiber, 165 mg sodium

a+ apple cheddar skewers

Hands-on Time: 4 MINUTES • *Hands-off Time:* NONE

I know a lot of people who love to eat apples and Cheddar in tandem. And I'm no different. One of my favorite 100-calorie afternoon snacks is a light string cheese and a small apple. It's well balanced and contains protein and calcium and is thus quite filling. So I created these skewers as a more festive version of this classic pairing. I love to serve it along with dessert when hosting a girls' night for my friends.

Be sure to thread the cheese onto the skewers gently to keep the cubes from breaking. I tend to use red-skinned apples because they're the most colorful, but any variety will be delicious. For even more variety, try the skewers with cut-up lowfat string cheese instead of the Cheddar.

1 medium apple, cored, seeded, and chopped into 1-inch chunks

1/4 teaspoon fresh lemon juice

1 ounce 75% light Cheddar, cut into 1/2-inch cubes (I used Cabot's)

2 decorative wooden skewers, about 10 inches long

In a small bowl, toss the apples with the lemon juice. Thread a piece of the apple onto a skewer, followed by cube of cheese. Continue skewering the remaining apples and cheese evenly among the 2 skewers. Serve immediately.

Makes 1 serving. 80 calories, 9 g protein, 6 g carbohydrates, 3 g fat, 2 g saturated fat, 10 mg cholesterol, <1 g fiber, 203 mg sodium

Quick Crunchy Potato Chips with Fixed-Up French Onion Dip (page 100)

quick crunchy potato chips

Hands-on Time: 9 MINUTES • *Hands-off Time:* NONE

These potato chips are shockingly fresh and tasty right from the microwave, and they're healthier than almost any chips on the market. Plus, they're likely to save you a lot of cash since baked chips tend to be quite expensive, yet large bags of fresh potatoes are not.

1 medium baking potato (7 to 8 ounces), scrubbed
1/2 teaspoon extra virgin olive oil
Sea salt, to taste
Olive oil spray

Slice the potato into very thin (about $1/16$-inch-thick) rounds. Place them in a large resealable plastic bag and drizzle the oil over them. Seal the bag and toss to evenly coat the potatoes. Season them with salt and toss again.

Cover a large microwave-safe dinner plate with parchment paper. Lightly mist the paper with spray. Working in batches if necessary, place the potato slices on the parchment in a single layer. Microwave the potatoes on high for 5 to 7 minutes, or until the chips are completely crisp (be careful not to burn them). Allow them to cool for about 2 minutes. Serve immediately.

Makes 2 servings. Each (about 3/4-ounce) serving has: 88 calories, 2 g protein, 17 g carbohydrates, 1 g fat, trace saturated fat, 0 mg cholesterol, 2 g fiber, 6 mg sodium

fixed-up french onion dip

Hands-on Time: 2 MINUTES •
Hands-off Time: 30 MINUTES FOR FLAVORS TO MELD, OPTIONAL

I've tried making onion dip with fat-free sour cream but just couldn't stomach it. The texture is just so off. On occasion I'd indulge by using light sour cream, but then I felt I had to be mindful of how much dip I was eating. Using a thick Greek yogurt, like Fage, I can finally eat as much dip as I want. Though it doesn't taste exactly like full-fat sour cream, it does provide the same texture and a great (though different) flavor.

Please note that depending on the brand of soup mix you use, the perfect amount will vary slightly. I'd start with 2 teaspoons and then continue adding, tasting as you do, until it suits your tastes. You can look for all-natural or organic onion soup mixes. I find the flavors differ significantly among brands, so try numerous brands if you don't love the first you try.

1 tablespoon onion soup mix, preferably an all-natural one, or to taste

1 (6-ounce) container fat-free plain Greek yogurt (I used Fage)

Add the onion soup mix directly to the container of yogurt. Stir well until thoroughly combined. Refrigerate for at least 30 minutes before serving (for best flavor), or up to 2 days. Serve with Quick Crunchy Potato Chips (see page 99), veggies, or whole-wheat pretzels for dipping.

Makes 2 servings. Each (heaping ¼-cup) serving has: 60 calories, 8 g protein, 7 g carbohydrates, trace fat, 0 g saturated fat, 0 mg cholesterol, 0 mg fiber, 225 mg sodium

margarita chips

Hands-on Time: 5 MINUTES • *Hands-off Time:* TIME TO PREHEAT OVEN

These insanely simple chips provide a very fresh twist to an otherwise packaged product. The idea comes from family friends of my test kitchen director, Stephanie. Over the years, she's attended a few of their "Parrot Head" Jimmy Buffett backyard barbecues. They love creating dishes that are margarita-inspired, and they always fry their own tortilla chips and sprinkle them with lime zest and salt. My version is healthier, not to mention much easier, as you don't have to stand over a pot of hot oil to cook batches of chips. When you make these, be sure to layer the lime with the chips in the bowl so it doesn't all end up at the bottom.

2 ounces baked tortilla chips (salted)
1 to 2 teaspoons freshly grated lime zest

Preheat the oven to 400°F.

Spread the chips in a single layer on a small baking sheet. Bake for 2 to 4 minutes, or until the chips are very warm.

Place about one-quarter of the chips in a medium serving bowl. Top with about one-quarter of the lime zest. Repeat with the remaining chips and lime zest. Serve immediately.

Makes 2 servings. Each (1-ounce) serving has: 110 calories, 2 g protein, 23 g carbohydrates, 1 g fat, 0 g saturated fat, 0 mg cholesterol, 1 g fiber, 65 mg sodium

wow 'em white bean dip

Hands-on Time: 7 MINUTES • *Hands-off Time:* NONE

I love dips because I think they "force" people to eat more veggies. Now that's great if the dip isn't doing more damage than the veggies are adding in health benefits, which is not the case with many dips. But fortunately, this is one that helps people eat more veggies and adds extra nutrients.

1 (15-ounce) can white beans (sometimes called cannellini beans or white kidney beans), rinsed and drained

1 medium garlic clove, coarsely chopped

1 tablespoon fresh lemon juice

1 tablespoon coarsely chopped parsley leaves

1 teaspoon extra virgin olive oil

2 tablespoons fat-free plain yogurt

1/8 teaspoon crushed red pepper flakes

Sea salt and pepper, to taste

In the bowl of a food processor fitted with a chopping blade, process the beans, garlic, lemon juice, and parsley until finely chopped (scrape down the sides of the bowl if necessary). With the processor on, stream in the olive oil and continue processing until the mixture is smooth. Spoon the mixture into a bowl and add the yogurt and red pepper flakes. Stir well to combine. Season with salt and pepper. Serve immediately with whole-grain crackers, veggies, or whole-wheat pita for dipping.

Makes 4 servings. Each (about a generous 1/4-cup) serving has: 101 calories, 5 g protein, 17 g carbohydrates, 2 g fat, trace saturated fat, trace cholesterol, 4 g fiber, 234 mg sodium

Asian Grilled London Broil

Luau London Broil

Mexican Cocktail Meatballs

Easy-As-Can-Be Pot Roast Supper

Boneless Pork "Ribs"

Simple Glazed Pork Chops

Cajun Pork Tenderloin with Tropical Salsa

Caramelized Apple Butter–Topped Pork Chops

Chicken Breasts with Goat Cheese & Fire-Roasted Tomatoes

Naked Chicken Parmesan

Crouton Breaded Chicken

Unbelievably Easy Chicken Parmesan

Balsamic Marinated Chicken

Presto Pesto Chicken

Roasted Rosemary Chicken

Turkey Cranberry Quesadilla

Grilled Turkey Cutlets with Cranberry Honey Mustard Sauce

Bacon-Wrapped Tilapia

Tandoori Tilapia

Grilled Salmon with Caramelized Onions

"Smoky" Salmon

Pan "Fried" Old Bay Salmon

Orange Shrimp

Buffalo Shrimp

Bruschettarogies

Cheddar Pierogies with Caramelized Onions

Pierogies with Kielbasa & Sauerkraut

Pierogies with Lemon Caper Butter

Breaded Portobello Mushrooms with Dijon

Penne and Asparagus with Ricotta Cheese

Ravio-sagne

Tuscan Pizza

Chicken Parmesan Pizza

Grilled Chicken, Goat Cheese, & Roasted Red Pepper Pizza

Salad Pizza with Grilled Chicken

Ravioli Soup

midsection-melting
main courses

asian grilled london broil

Hands-on Time: 4 MINUTES •
Hands-off Time: 15 MINUTES TO REST PLUS 8 TO 10 MINUTES TO GRILL PLUS 10 ADDITIONAL MINUTES TO REST

This London broil really couldn't be easier, especially if you buy the meat already trimmed. If your grocery store sells it with a big layer of fat, save time by asking the butcher to trim it for you while you shop. They don't charge for this service at most major grocery stores (though they don't decrease the price to reflect the new weight, either).

Though I always love the flavor an outdoor grill provides, as a second option, this dish can be prepared under a broiler for 4 to 5 minutes per side for medium-rare, or until the desired doneness is reached.

1³/4 pounds trimmed London broil

1 teaspoon extra virgin olive oil

1 tablespoon Asian spice rub (see Note), or to taste (I used McCormick Far East Sesame Ginger Blend)

Salt, to taste

Rub the London broil evenly on all sides with the olive oil, followed by the spice rub. Preheat a grill to high heat.

Let the London broil stand for 15 minutes. Grill it for 4 to 5 minutes per side for medium-rare, or until desired doneness is reached. Transfer it to a serving platter and place a sheet of aluminum foil loosely over the top (of the meat, not the whole platter). Allow it to rest for 10 minutes, and then slice it very thinly against the grain. Serve immediately. Refrigerate and enjoy any leftovers for up to 3 days.

NOTE There are tons of spice rubs sold in cans and jars these days. You can literally use any that says Asian, Szechuan, Japanese, etc. If you are using a rub with no salt, you'll definitely want to add a bit.

Makes 6 servings. Each (about 4-ounce) serving has: 135 calories, 28 g protein, 0 g carbohydrates, 5 g fat, 2 g saturated fat, 58 mg cholesterol, 0 g fiber, 284 mg sodium

luau london broil

Hands-on Time: 8 MINUTES •
Hands-off Time: 4 to 6 HOURS (OR OVERNIGHT) TO MARINATE PLUS 10 MINUTES
TO GRILL PLUS 10 MINUTES TO REST

This London broil has a wonderfully subtle flavor and is particularly great for folks who love mild foods. Though, unlike the other London broil recipes in this book, it doesn't make the best sandwich leftovers. The leftovers are, however, great for salads, rice bowls, or other Asian-inspired favorites.

Though I always love the added flavor that an outdoor grill provides, as a second option, this London broil can be prepared under a broiler for 4 to 5 minutes per side for medium-rare, or longer until the desired doneness is reached.

1/3 cup lower-sodium soy sauce
1 tablespoon fresh lemon or lime juice
1 1/2 tablespoons peeled, minced fresh ginger
1 tablespoon brown sugar, not packed
1 teaspoon extra virgin olive oil
1 3/4 pounds trimmed London broil

In a medium bowl, whisk together the soy sauce, lemon or lime juice, ginger, sugar, and olive oil until well combined. Place the London broil in a large resealable plastic bag and pour the marinade over the meat. Seal the bag and toss the meat well to coat it completely with the marinade. Refrigerate for at least 4 to 6 hours or overnight.

Preheat the grill to high heat.

Remove the London broil from the bag and drain off any excess marinade. Grill for about 5 minutes per side for medium-rare, or until desired doneness is reached. Transfer to a plate and tent with foil. Allow the meat to rest for 10 minutes. Slice against the grain into thin slices and serve immediately, or refrigerate to enjoy as leftovers for up to 3 days.

Makes 6 servings. Each (about 4-ounce) serving has: 137 calories, 28 g protein, <1 g carbohydrates, 4 g fat, 2 g saturated fat, 58 mg cholesterol, trace fiber, 194 mg sodium

mexican cocktail meatballs

Hands-on Time: 10 MINUTES • *Hands-off Time:* 7 to 9 MINUTES

These meatballs are great as a party appetizer served with pretty toothpicks for munching or excellent as a quick weeknight dinner served over brown or Mexican rice. If you have trouble finding Mexican seasoning, you can substitute lower-sodium taco seasoning. If you are serving them at a cocktail party, you might consider tossing them in only half of the sauce and adding the remaining sauce to a small bowl for dipping.

Save time by having your children roll the meatballs. It's fun for them and will give you more "you time." The next day, save even more time by using the leftovers as the meat for throw-together tacos using soft corn tortillas.

Olive oil spray
1 pound 96% lean ground beef
2 ounces shredded 75% light Cheddar (I used Cabot's)
1 tablespoon plus 1 teaspoon Mexican seasoning (I used McCormick)
1/4 cup mild, medium, or hot red chili enchilada sauce, warmed

Preheat the oven to 400°F. Lightly mist a large nonstick baking sheet with spray.

In a medium bowl, mix the beef, cheese, and seasoning until well combined. Divide the mixture into 24 portions and roll each into a ball about 1¹/2 inches in diameter. Place them on a baking sheet or pan so they don't touch and bake them for 7 to 9 minutes, or until they are no longer pink inside. Transfer the meatballs to a medium serving bowl and pour the sauce over top. Toss and serve immediately.

Makes 4 servings. Each (6 meatballs with sauce) serving has: 166 calories, 27 g protein, 1 g carbohydrates, 6 g fat, 2 g saturated fat, 65 mg cholesterol, 0 g fiber, 421 mg sodium

easy-as-can-be pot roast supper

Hands-on Time: 9 MINUTES •
Hands-off Time: TIME TO PREHEAT OVEN PLUS 30 TO 40 MINUTES

I love using tiny potatoes and baby carrots, which makes this recipe insanely easy. That said, sometimes tiny potatoes cost a minor fortune. If that's the case, save money by using larger boiling potatoes. You'll have to spend time cutting them into cubes, but it might make sense.

You don't have to use the nonstick foil here if you have a really good nonstick roasting pan, but it makes cleanup almost nonexistent, so I swear by it.

1^{1}/2 pounds baby carrots

2 pounds red or white potatoes, cut into 1-inch cubes

1 tablespoon plus 2 teaspoons extra virgin olive oil, divided

Sea salt and pepper

One 1^{3}/4-pound trimmed top round roast

5^{1}/2-ounce can tomato juice (I used Campbell's)

2 teaspoons dried thyme

2 medium onions, trimmed, peeled, and cut into quarters

Preheat the oven to 450°F. Line a large roasting pan with nonstick aluminum foil. Add the carrots and potatoes. Drizzle 1 tablespoon plus 1 teaspoon of the olive oil over the vegetables and season them with salt and pepper. Toss just to combine, then distribute them in an even layer in the bottom of the pan, leaving room for the roast in the center.

Rub the roast all over with the remaining 1 teaspoon olive oil, then season it with ^{1}/4 teaspoon salt and ^{1}/4 teaspoon pepper. Set it in the center of the veggies and pour the juice evenly over all. Sprinkle the thyme over the top. Roast the meat, carrots, and potatoes for 18 minutes. Then, stir the potatoes and carrots (if using nonstick foil, be careful not to tear it). Separate the onion quarters into pieces. Scatter them over the potatoes and carrots. Continue roasting until a meat thermometer inserted in the center of the roast reads 125°F; for medium rare, about 15 to 20 minutes more.

Carefully transfer the roast to a platter. Loosely tent the roast with foil for 10 minutes while the juices redistribute internally. If the veggies are not tender, rotate them one more time and continue roasting, up to 10 minutes more.

Slice the meat into thin slices against the grain and serve immediately with the veggies.

Makes 6 servings. Each (about 4 ounces beef plus 2 cups vegetables) serving has: 345 calories, 33 g protein, 42 g carbohydrates, 8 g fat, 2 g saturated fat, 58 mg cholesterol, 7 g fiber, 310 mg sodium

boneless pork "ribs"

Hands-on Time: 10 MINUTES •
Hands-off Time: 6 HOURS OR OVERNIGHT TO MARINATE
PLUS TIME TO PREHEAT OVEN

Because pork tenderloin is so tender, this dish will taste fattier than it is. Granted, you never want to overcook any meat, or it will be tough. I used the spare rib sauce most commonly found in my area and that I believe to be the most common across the country (look for it in the international section of your grocery store next to the soy and hoisin sauces). You may note that the sauce itself is extremely high in sodium. Though you marinate these "ribs" in 2 tablespoons of sauce, only half of that gets consumed in the finished dish. The result may not be low in sodium, but you still could be saving up to 75 percent of the sodium you'd consume in the traditional dish.

Please note that "8 ounces trimmed boneless pork tenderloin" means the weight after trimming. Thus, you should buy a bigger piece. "Eight ounces boneless pork tenderloin, trimmed" means you should buy an 8-ounce piece and then trim it.

8 ounces trimmed boneless pork tenderloin
2 tablespoons spare rib sauce (I used Lee
    Kum Kee)
Olive oil spray

Slice the pork crosswise into 8 equal medallions (about 1 ounce each). Toss the pork with sauce in a medium resealable plastic container to coat them well. Cover and refrigerate at least 6 hours or overnight.

Preheat the broiler. Line a small baking sheet with nonstick aluminum foil and lightly mist the foil with spray.

Remove the pork from the sauce, allowing any excess to drip off. Place the ribs on the baking sheet in a single layer so they do not touch. Using your fingers, gently shape the medallions into long, thin (about 1-inch-wide) strips.

Broil on the top oven rack for 2 minutes. Flip the strips and continue cooking until just barely pink inside, about 1 to 2 minutes more. Serve immediately.

Makes 2 servings. Each (4-strip) serving has: 145 calories, 24 g protein, 4 g carbohydrates, 3 g fat, <1 g saturated fat, 74 mg cholesterol, trace fiber, 480 mg sodium

simple glazed pork chops

Hands-on Time: 9 MINUTES • *Hands-off Time:* TIME TO PREHEAT BROILER

Not only is this recipe incredibly easy, but cleanup consists of throwing away a piece of foil if you line your pan with nonstick foil.

I've found that folks have a tendency to overcook pork. Though there was a time everyone thought it had to be nearly overcooked, it's now been found safe to eat if a little less done—by which, I mean cooked with just the faintest hint of pink (as in just barely pink, not actually fully pink) in the center. You still never want to eat raw pork.

The first time you make this recipe, you may want to buy an extra chop to "play with." I've found that broiler intensity varies significantly from oven to oven, so it's tough to give you the precise time on this one. But timing really does matter here, as the chop needs to be cooked through on the inside before the sauce burns. Once you figure out the perfect timing with that one chop, you'll always know exactly how long to broil your pork chops, whether you're making this recipe or another broiled pork chop recipe. So it really is worth a one-time effort that will take less than 10 minutes.

Olive oil spray (from a spray bottle, not a store-bought, prefilled one that contains propellant; I used a Misto)

2 tablespoons ketchup

1$\frac{1}{2}$ tablespoons brown sugar, not packed

2 (4-ounce) trimmed, boneless pork chops, about $\frac{3}{4}$ inch thick (3$\frac{1}{2}$ to 4$\frac{1}{2}$-ounce chops are okay)

$\frac{1}{4}$ teaspoon garlic powder

Sea salt and pepper, to taste

Preheat the broiler. Line a small baking sheet with nonstick aluminum foil. Lightly mist the foil with spray.

In a small bowl, mix the ketchup and brown sugar until well combined.

Lightly mist both sides of the chops with spray, and then season them with garlic powder, salt, and pepper. Place the chops side by side on the prepared baking sheet, not touching. Broil the chops about 2 minutes. Flip them and broil 1 more minute. Brush half of the ketchup mixture evenly over the top of each and continue broiling until the glaze caramelizes (browns) and the pork just barely has a hint of pink inside, 1 to 2 minutes more. Serve immediately.

Makes 2 servings. Each (1-chop) serving has: 173 calories, 23 g protein, 11 g carbohydrates, 4 g fat, 1 g saturated fat, 65 mg cholesterol, trace fiber, 218 mg sodium

cajun pork tenderloin with tropical salsa

Hands-on Time: 12 MINUTES •
Hands-off Time: 15 MINUTES TO MARINATE PLUS 16 to 18 MINUTES
PLUS 10 MINUTES TO REST

Many Cajun seasonings list salt as the first ingredient on the label. Try to avoid buying one of those, if possible. It's much better to be able to season your food as much as you like without it being overloaded with salt, especially if you're like me and like spicy or super-flavorful food.

This recipe is great with pretty much any tropical salsa, so just pick one that seems good to you. I definitely prefer the fresh ones that are most often found in the produce section of grocery stores. But if it's inconvenient to hunt one of those down, you can use a jarred one.

1¼ pounds trimmed pork tenderloin

1 teaspoon extra virgin olive oil

2 teaspoons Cajun or blackened seasoning, or more to taste

Olive oil spray

1 tablespoon honey

1⅓ cups papaya mango, pineapple, or any other tropical salsa, preferably fresh (I used Trader Joe's Papaya Mango Salsa)

Preheat the oven to 350°F.

Rub the tenderloin evenly with the olive oil. Then rub the Cajun seasoning evenly over it. Let it stand for 15 minutes.

Heat a large ovenproof nonstick skillet over medium-high heat. When the pan is hot, lightly mist it with spray. Cook the tenderloin until it is just browned all over, 4 to 5 minutes. Remove it from the heat. Using a pastry brush or your fingers, rub the honey evenly over the tenderloin. If one end is very narrow, tuck it under to make it an equal thickness with the rest of the tenderloin. Transfer the pan to the oven and cook the tenderloin (uncovered) until there is just a hint of pink inside or a meat thermometer reaches 155°F, 16 to 18 minutes.

Remove the tenderloin from the oven and immediately place a sheet of foil loosely over it (not over the whole pan). Allow it to sit for 10 minutes. Transfer the tenderloin to a cutting board. Holding your knife at a 45-degree angle, slice it into thin slices. Serve immediately with salsa.

Makes 4 servings. Each (4 ounces pork plus ⅓ cup salsa) serving has: 222 calories, 30 g protein, 12 g carbohydrates, 4 g fat, 1 g saturated fat, 92 mg cholesterol, 0 g fiber, 809 mg sodium

caramelized apple butter–topped pork chops

Hands-on Time: 9 MINUTES • *Hands-off Time:* TIME TO PREHEAT BROILER

I'm repeating this headnote from the recipe for Simple Glazed Pork Chops (page 111) because it's really important: I've found that folks tend to overcook pork. Though there was a time everyone thought it had to be nearly overcooked, it's now been found safe to eat it a little less done—by which I mean with just the very faintest hint of pink (as in just barely pink, not actually fully pink) in the center. You never want to eat raw pork.

Also, the first time you make this recipe you may want to buy an extra chop to "play with." I've found broiler intensity varies significantly from oven to oven, so it's tough to give you the precise time on this one. And timing really does matter here, as the chop needs to be cooked through on the inside before the sauce burns. Once you figure out the perfect timing with that one chop, you'll always know exactly how long to broil your pork chops, whether you're making this recipe or one of the other broiled pork chop recipes. So it really is worth a one-time effort that will take less than 10 minutes.

When purchasing apple butter, look for it next to the peanut butter and jelly in your grocery store.

Olive oil spray (from a spray bottle, not a store-bought, prefilled one that contains propellant; I used a Misto)

2 (3- to 4-ounce) trimmed, boneless pork chops, about 3/4 inch thick

1/4 teaspoon garlic powder

Sea salt and fresh ground black pepper, to taste

2 tablespoons apple butter, preferably a natural one (I used Eden), divided

Preheat the broiler. Line a small baking sheet with nonstick aluminum foil and lightly mist the foil with spray.

Lightly mist the chops all over with spray, and then season them with the garlic, salt, and pepper. Place them side by side on the prepared baking sheet, not touching. Transfer the sheet to the top oven rack and broil the chops about 3 minutes. Flip them and brush 1 tablespoon of the apple butter evenly over the top of each chop. Continue broiling until the apple butter caramelizes (turns brown in spots) and the pork just barely has a hint of pink inside, 2 to 4 minutes. Serve immediately.

Makes 2 servings. Each (1-chop) serving has: 164 calories, 22 g protein, 8 g carbohydrates, 4 g fat, 1 g saturated fat, 65 mg cholesterol, trace fiber, 51 mg sodium

chicken breasts with goat cheese and fire-roasted tomatoes

Hands-on Time: 7 MINUTES • *Hands-off Time:* 5 to 9 MINUTES

This dish is exceptionally easy to make and worth every second. That said, there is one thing to note: Be careful when checking the chicken for doneness. The tomatoes will likely drip into the chicken. If you cut into the chicken or poke it with a fork to test for doneness, be sure it's not the liquid from the tomatoes making the chicken look pink even if it's not.

4 (4-ounce) trimmed boneless, skinless chicken breasts
Sea salt and pepper, to taste
Olive oil spray
1/2 cup canned, drained, diced fire-roasted tomatoes or fire-roasted tomatoes with garlic
2 ounces (about 1/2 cup) goat cheese crumbles
2 tablespoons finely slivered fresh basil leaves, or more to taste (optional)

Preheat the oven to 350°F.

Season the chicken with salt and pepper.

Place a medium ovenproof nonstick skillet over high heat. When it's hot, lightly mist the skillet with spray and immediately add the chicken side by side to the pan so it does not touch. Cook the chicken just until it is golden brown on the outsides, 1 to 2 minutes per side.

Remove the pan from the heat and top each piece of chicken evenly with about 2 table-spoons of the tomatoes, followed by about 1/2 ounce of the cheese. Transfer the skillet to the oven and bake the chicken until it is no longer pink inside and the cheese is melted, 5 to 9 minutes. Top evenly with the basil, if desired. Serve immediately.

Makes 4 servings. Each (1 topped breast) serving has: 171 calories, 29 g protein, 2 g carbohy-drates, 4 g fat, 2 g saturated fat, 72 mg cholesterol, trace fiber, 198 mg sodium

naked chicken parmesan

Hands-on Time: 9 MINUTES •
Hands-off Time: 27 to 30 MINUTES PLUS 5 MINUTES TO REST

Everyone who knows me knows chicken parmesan was one of the major reasons I was overweight. Though I certainly don't eat the deep-fried version these days, I do still love the incredible combination of tender chicken, perfectly seasoned marinara sauce, and gooey cheese. Here is one of the all-time easiest versions that's especially great for low-carbers, as it's not breaded. If you prefer the more traditional breaded chicken parmesan, I have a quick answer for you too: Just pop over to page 118 and try the Unbelievably Easy Chicken Parmesan. Or, better yet, try both!

4 (4-ounce) trimmed boneless, skinless
   chicken breasts
Sea salt and pepper, to taste
Garlic powder, to taste
1 cup low-fat jarred marinara sauce (lower-
   sodium, if possible), divided
4 ounces (about 1 1/4 cups) finely shredded
   low-fat mozzarella cheese (no more
   than 3 g of fat per ounce; I used Lucerne,
   found at Safeway chains)
1/2 teaspoon garlic powder
2 tablespoons finely slivered fresh basil
   leaves, plus more to taste

Preheat the oven to 350°F.

Lay the chicken breasts on a flat work surface between two sheets of waxed paper or plastic wrap. Pound them with the flat side of a meat mallet, working from the center outward, until they are an even 1/2 inch thick throughout. Season with sea salt, pepper, and garlic powder to taste.

Spread 1/3 cup of the marinara sauce in the bottom of an 8 × 8-inch glass baking dish. Lay the chicken breasts side by side over the marinara sauce. Spoon the remaining 2/3 cup sauce evenly over the chicken breasts to cover them. Cover the dish with foil and bake for 15 minutes. Remove the foil and sprinkle the cheese evenly over the chicken breasts followed by 1/2 teaspoon garlic powder. Continue cooking the chicken (uncovered) for 12 to 15 more minutes, or until the chicken is no longer pink inside. Remove it from the oven and sprinkle the basil leaves over the top. Let stand 5 minutes, then serve immediately.

Makes 4 servings. Each (1 chicken breast) serving has: 210 calories, 35 g protein, 7 g carbohydrates, 4 g fat, 1 g saturated fat, 76 mg cholesterol, 2 g fiber, 445 mg sodium

crouton breaded chicken

Hands-on Time: 8 MINUTES •
Hands-off Time: 6 HOURS OR OVERNIGHT TO MARINATE PLUS TIME TO PREHEAT OVEN PLUS 8 TO 10 MINUTES

Soaking chicken in buttermilk is an amazing, guilt-free way to make it super-tender and juicy. I've converted more folks to unfried chicken by soaking the chicken in buttermilk than I could possibly recall. Just be sure you don't overcook the chicken. If you do, not only will the chicken not be plump and juicy, the juice that should have been inside will run out and make the breading soggy.

2 (4-ounce) trimmed boneless, skinless chicken breasts, pounded to 1/2-inch thickness

1/3 cup reduced-fat buttermilk

Olive oil spray (from a spray bottle, not a store-bought, prefilled one that contains propellant; I used a Misto)

1 ounce (about 24 fat-free herb-seasoned croutons (I used Marie Callender's Fat-Free Herb-Seasoned Croutons)

Place the chicken breasts in a medium resealable plastic bag. Pour the buttermilk over them and seal the bag. Let them soak 6 hours or overnight, turning once or twice.

Preheat the oven to 450°F. Lightly mist a small nonstick baking pan or sheet with spray.

Add the croutons to a resealable plastic bag. Pound them with the flat side of a meat mallet until crushed into very fine crumbs. Transfer the crumbs to a medium shallow bowl.

Remove one breast from the bag and let any excess buttermilk drip off. Dip it into the crumbs, rotating it to cover the breast completely. Place the breaded breast on the prepared baking sheet. Repeat with the second breast and place it on the baking sheet so the breasts don't touch. If crumbs remain, press them into the tops of the breasts. Lightly spray the tops of the breasts with spray. Bake them 5 minutes, and then carefully, being sure not to remove the coating, flip them. Lightly mist the tops with spray and continue to bake for another 3 to 5 minutes, or until the coating is crisp and the chicken is no longer pink inside. Serve immediately.

Makes 2 servings. Each serving has: 195 calories, 29 g protein, 11 g carbohydrates, 2 g fat, <1 g saturated fat, 67 mg cholesterol, 0 g fiber, 265 mg sodium

unbelievably easy chicken parmesan

Hands-on Time: 12 MINUTES •
Hands-off Time: 6 HOURS TO MARINATE PLUS 8 to 12 MINUTES

Rarely do I shock myself with how great a made-over dish can taste. I'm pretty realistic. Apple pie is pretty much an impossibility if I want it to taste like traditional pie and be lower in fat and calories because of all of the butter. There really is no substitute for butter in a traditional pie crust.

I thought this dish would be an impossibility as well. But when we pulled the chicken out of the oven the first time, everyone in my test kitchen was shocked at how fattening it tasted. We knew it would be good, but we had no idea it would actually be great, especially given how much quicker it is than the traditional version! Just be sure you don't overcook the chicken. If you do, not only will the chicken be dry, the breading will fall off.

1 recipe Crouton Breaded Chicken (page 117)
¼ cup low-fat marinara sauce (lower-sodium, if possible)
½ ounce (2½ tablespoons) finely shredded reduced-fat mozzarella cheese (no more than 3 g of fat per ounce; I used Lucerne, found at Safeway chains)
1 teaspoon grated reduced-fat Parmesan cheese (look for it in a plastic canister or jar, not in the refrigerated section)

Follow the directions for the Crouton Breaded Chicken, using fat-free Italian or Caesar-seasoned croutons instead of the herb-seasoned ones if you can find them (if you can't, the herb-seasoned ones are a great second choice). During the last 2 minutes of baking, top each chicken breast with half of the sauce, half of the mozzarella, and half of the parmesan. Bake until the sauce is warm, the cheese is melted, and the chicken is cooked through. Serve immediately.

Makes 2 servings. Each serving has: 228 calories, 31 g protein, 14 g carbohydrates, 3 g fat, <1 g saturated fat, 70 mg cholesterol, 1 g fiber, 419 mg sodium

Unbelievably Easy Chicken Parmesan
with Balsamic Roasted Asparagus (page 168)

balsamic marinated chicken

Hands-on Time: 5 MINUTES •
Hands-off Time: 6 HOURS OR OVERNIGHT TO MARINATE, PLUS TIME TO PREHEAT
OVEN PLUS 10 MINUTES TO GRILL

If you're a big fan of balsamic vinegar, you'll love this chicken. And if you're able to treat yourself, you might consider hunting down a really great aged balsamic. It will turn this no-brainer recipe into something pretty extraordinary. But whether you do that or just grab the one on sale at the grocery store, the result is sure to be delicious.

2 tablespoons light balsamic vinaigrette (no more than 2 g of fat per tablespoon; I used Newman's Own Light Balsamic Vinaigrette)

2 tablespoons balsamic vinegar

1 teaspoon freshly ground black pepper

1 teaspoon dried rosemary leaves

4 (4-ounce) trimmed boneless, skinless chicken breasts

In a medium resealable container, mix the vinaigrette, vinegar, pepper, and rosemary. Add the chicken and rotate it to cover it in the marinade. Refrigerate it at least 6 hours or overnight, rotating at least once.

Preheat a grill to high heat.

Grill the chicken until no longer pink inside, about 5 minutes per side.

Makes 4 servings. Each (1 chicken breast) serving has: 137 calories, 26 g protein, 1 g carbohydrates, 2 g fat, trace saturated fat, 66 mg cholesterol, trace fiber, 149 mg sodium

presto pesto chicken

Hands-on Time: 3 MINUTES •
Hands-off Time: TIME TO PREHEAT OVEN PLUS 8 TO 9 MINUTES

I love pesto, but unfortunately, it's typically made with a shocking amount of oil and is thus very fattening. Luckily, I've discovered other ways to enjoy the flavor of pesto without the fat and calories. Using herbs from a tube or frozen herbs works really well on this chicken to give it that classic pesto flavor without the fat . . . and without a lot of work.

Please note that if you buy frozen herbs, you should measure them out yourself before using them in recipes. I've found that a 1-teaspoon block of herbs is rarely an actual teaspoon.

½ teaspoon Gourmet Garden Garlic Blend or frozen herbs (look for Gourmet Garden in tubes in the produce section or frozen herbs at Trader Joe's)

1 teaspoon Gourmet Garden Basil Herb Blend (look for Gourmet Garden in tubes in the produce section or frozen herbs at Trader Joe's)

1 (4-ounce) Basic Grilled Chicken breast (see page 219) or lean, store-bought grilled chicken breast

1 heaping tablespoon (about ¼ ounce) finely shredded reduced-fat mozzarella cheese (no more than 3 g of fat per ounce; I used Lucerne, found at Safeway chains)

Preheat the oven to 400°F.

In a small bowl, stir the garlic and basil blends and ¼ teaspoon water until well combined. Place the chicken in the center of a large piece of foil. Spread the garlic mixture evenly over the top of the chicken breast. Create a pouch by folding the foil loosely over the chicken and then folding the ends together to seal them tightly (be sure the foil is not touching the top of the chicken, so as not to disturb the sauce).

Place the foil directly on an oven rack and bake for 3 minutes. Carefully unwrap the foil and sprinkle the cheese evenly over the top of the chicken, and then rewrap the pouch. Continue baking an additional 5 to 6 minutes, or until the chicken is warmed through and the cheese is melted. Serve immediately.

Makes 1 serving. 168 calories, 28 protein, 2 g carbohydrates, 3 g fat, <1 g saturated fat, 68 mg cholesterol, trace fiber, 350 mg sodium

roasted rosemary chicken

Hands-on Time: 7 MINUTES •
Hands-off Time: TIME TO PREHEAT OVEN PLUS 4 TO 6 MINUTES

I've heard a lot of people comment over the years that white-meat chicken is dry. True, it's not as fatty as dark meat, but it's not dry when it's cooked properly. The important thing to remember is that as soon as it's no longer pink inside, you want to get it off the heat. If you don't see pink, it's cooked. You don't need to cook it another five minutes "just to be sure." All that will do is dry it out. Additionally, it's important that you start cooking it at a high heat and don't overcrowd it in the pan. If the heat isn't high enough or the pan is too small for the amount of chicken, excess moisture will build up and you won't get that browning on the outside that is so delicious. These basic tips, along with misting or very lightly rubbing chicken breasts with olive oil to create a protective coating of sorts, will keep you from needing tons of fat to make absolutely scrumptious chicken dishes.

2 (4-ounce) trimmed boneless, skinless
    chicken breasts
1/2 teaspoon extra virgin olive oil
1/4 teaspoon garlic powder
1/4 teaspoon dried rosemary
Sea salt and pepper, to taste

Preheat the oven to 350°F.

In a medium bowl, toss the chicken breasts with the olive oil, and then season both sides with the garlic powder, rosemary, salt, and pepper.

Place a medium ovenproof nonstick skillet over high heat. When it's hot, add the chicken and sear 1 to 2 minutes per side, or until the chicken is golden brown on the outside. Transfer the pan to the oven and bake the chicken until it is no longer pink inside, 4 to 6 minutes.

Makes 2 servings. Each (1 chicken breast) serving has: 137 calories, 26 g protein, trace carbohydrates, 3 g fat, <1 g saturated fat, 66 mg cholesterol, trace fiber, 74 mg sodium

turkey cranberry quesadilla

Hands-on Time: 8 MINUTES • *Hands-off Time:* 4 TO 7 MINUTES

I always try to buy jarred cranberry sauce, as it generally lasts longer than canned and tends to contain more natural ingredients. If you can't find jarred, it's okay to buy canned because it freezes well. Simply use what you need and then portion out the rest to save in small resealable freezer bags for future use.

You can save even more time on this recipe by buying precooked turkey breast strips, though you should be careful they haven't been cooked in too much fat or have too much added sodium.

If you can't find raw turkey breast strips, ask your butcher to cut a turkey breast or turkey cutlet for you. He or she is likely to do it at no extra charge.

3 ounces raw turkey breast strips

Salt and pepper, to taste

Olive oil spray

1 (about 8-inch-diameter) reduced-fat, whole-wheat flour tortilla

1 tablespoon jarred or canned cranberry sauce

1½ ounces (about ¾ cup) finely shredded 75% light Cheddar cheese (I used Cabot's)

1 teaspoon seeded and finely chopped jalapeño (optional)

Preheat the oven to 350°F.

In a small bowl, toss the turkey with salt and pepper.

Place a small nonstick skillet over high heat. When hot, lightly mist the pan with spray and add the turkey. Cook the strips, rotating them occasionally, until lightly browned and no longer pink inside, 2 to 4 minutes. Set aside.

Place the tortilla on a small nonstick baking sheet. Using the back of a spoon, spread the cranberry sauce evenly over half the tortilla. Sprinkle half the cheese evenly over the top of the sauce, followed by the turkey, the jalapeño (if desired), and then the remaining cheese. Fold the bare half over the filling. Bake the quesadilla until the cheese is melted, 4 to 7 minutes. Using a spatula, flip it onto a clean, dry cutting board. Slice it into 4 wedges. Transfer the wedges to a serving plate and serve immediately.

Makes 1 quesadilla. 318 calories, 38 g protein, 30 g carbohydrates, 6 g fat, 2 g saturated fat, 49 mg cholesterol, 2 g fiber, 517 mg sodium

grilled turkey cutlets with cranberry honey mustard sauce

Hands-on Time: 8 MINUTES • *Hands-off Time:* TIME TO PREHEAT GRILL

I love making turkey cutlets, especially when I'm in a hurry, because they generally require very little trimming and cook exceptionally quickly. Whether you pan "fry" them or grill them, as I have done here, they take only a couple of minutes per side. After basic preparation, I always like to add a simple sauce. I could have thrown together another salsa suggestion here, but wanted to be a bit more creative with this one. And I've gone to upscale sandwich shops and cafés and ordered turkey sandwiches spread with cranberries and sweet mustard or mayonnaise, so I thought that might be a great place to start. I was very pleased very quickly, and I think you will be too.

1/4 cup canned cranberry sauce with whole cranberries
1 tablespoon plus 1 teaspoon honey mustard
1 teaspoon extra virgin olive oil
1 pound trimmed boneless, skinless turkey cutlets
Sea salt and pepper, to taste

Preheat a grill over high heat.

In a small bowl, mix the cranberry sauce and mustard until well combined. Cover the bowl with a paper towel and microwave on high in 15-second intervals until the mixture is hot and begins to thin slightly, about 30 seconds total. Stir again to combine.

Rub the oil and then the salt and pepper evenly over both sides of each cutlet. Grill the cutlets about 1 minute per side, or until no longer pink in the center. Transfer them to a large plate or platter and top evenly with the sauce. Serve immediately.

Makes 4 servings. Each (about 3 1/2 ounces turkey plus about 1 1/2 tablespoons sauce) serving has: 167 calories, 28 g protein, 9 g carbohydrates, 2 g fat, trace saturated fat, 45 mg cholesterol, trace fiber, 146 mg sodium

Grilled Turkey Cutlets with Cranberry Honey Mustard Sauce
with Super-Speedy Sweet Potatoes (page 158)

bacon-wrapped tilapia

Hands-on Time: 5 MINUTES •
Hands-off Time: TIME TO PREHEAT BROILER PLUS 8 TO 12 MINUTES

I've encountered many people who are shocked that I eat real pork bacon, being that I've kept off fifty-five pounds for close to twenty years. Others are shocked that I include it in my cookbooks. The interesting thing to realize is that center-cut bacon—real pork bacon that's 35 to 40 percent leaner than other pork bacon—is often as lean as most turkey bacon, yet it tastes like real bacon because it is. The flavor is much stronger than turkey bacon and doesn't have that turkey aftertaste many brands of turkey bacon do.

When buying fish, I often opt for frozen individually wrapped fillets. They're usually fresher than those I find at the fish counter, and I buy them when they go on sale so I can always have some handy in my freezer.

Olive oil spray
2 (about 4 ounces each) or 4 (about
    2 ounces each) tilapia fillets
Sea salt and pepper, to taste
Garlic powder, to taste
4 slices center-cut bacon

Preheat the broiler. Line a small baking sheet with nonstick aluminum foil. Lightly mist the foil with spray.

If using 2-ounce fillets, stack them in pairs, smooth sides together, creating 2 4-ounce "fillets." Season both sides of each fillet with garlic powder, salt, and pepper. Starting at the narrower end of one of the fillets (or fillet couplings), wrap 2 of the bacon strips around the tilapia so they cover as much surface area of the fish as possible. Repeat with the remaining fillet (or fillet coupling) and bacon.

Broil until the bacon is cooked and the fish flakes easily, 5 to 6 minutes per side. Serve immediately.

Makes 2 servings. Each serving has: 133 calories, 25 g protein, 0 g carbohydrates, 6 g fat, 3 g saturated fat, 70 mg cholesterol, 0 g fiber, 306 mg sodium

Bacon-Wrapped Tilapia with
Italian Herbed Zucchini (page 176)

tandoori tilapia

Hands-on Time: 6 MINUTES • *Hands-off Time:* NONE

Tandoori is actually a cooking method, not an ingredient. In traditional Indian cuisine, the term describes a marinated meat cooked over an intense fire in a tandoor—a clay oven containing a hot fire. But we now commonly associate it with a type of marinade. Today, you can find tandoori paste in most grocery stores. It has intense flavor (which I love). By mixing it with yogurt, you cut some of the sodium and make a great simple marinade for fish, chicken, and many other meats.

1 tablespoon jarred tandoori paste (look for it in the international section with Indian curry; if you can't find tandoori, mild red curry paste is a second choice)

2 tablespoons fat-free plain yogurt

2 (about 4 ounces each) or 4 (about 2 ounces each) tilapia fillets

Olive oil spray

1 small lime, cut into wedges

In a small bowl, stir the tandoori paste and yogurt until well combined. Brush the fillets evenly on both sides with the mixture.

Set a medium nonstick skillet over high heat (if preparing 4 fillets, use a large skillet). When hot, lightly mist it with spray. Add the fish to the pan and cook for 1 to 2 minutes per side, or until it's no longer translucent and flakes easily. Squeeze the lime wedges over the fillets and serve immediately.

Makes 2 servings. Each serving has: 120 calories, 23 g protein, 1 g carbohydrates, 2 g fat, <1 g saturated fat, 57 mg cholesterol, 0 g fiber, 258 mg sodium

grilled salmon with caramelized onions

Hands-on Time: 10 MINUTES (ONIONS MUST BE MADE IN ADVANCE) •
Hands-off Time: TIME TO PREHEAT GRILL

I recently ate dinner at the home of a couple who are producers-turned-friends, Barry and Jen. They work in food TV, so they're all about great-tasting food. When I showed up, they were making a huge pan of caramelized onions that looked unbelievably good. They were serving them with almost everything that night, which I was happy about because I love onions.

I have to admit I was surprised when I saw them piling the onions on grilled salmon. It was not a combination I'd ever considered. But because when in Rome you're supposed to do as the Romans do, I dug in. It was delicious! I came home and figured out how to make caramelized onions that didn't need a lot of fat or hands-on time. This dish is now a favorite among many I've served.

Although salmon is high in fat, it's good-for-you fat when eaten in moderation. Wild salmon has 12 fewer calories and 1.5 grams less fat per ounce than farm-raised, so I always try to buy that. But it is more expensive and tougher to find. So if you choose farm-raised, it will add 47 calories and 5 grams of fat per serving to this dish.

Olive oil spray (from a spray bottle, not a store-bought, prefilled one that contains propellant; I used a Misto)

2 (4-ounce) skinless salmon fillets, preferably wild-caught

Sea salt and pepper, to taste

2/3 cup Easier-Than-Caramelized Onions (see page 225), reheated if necessary

Preheat a grill to high.

Lightly mist both sides of each salmon fillet with spray. Season with salt and pepper. Lightly mist a large sheet of aluminum foil and place it directly on the grill rack, spray side up. Set the fillets side by side on the foil so they do not touch. Grill them until the salmon is cooked through, 2 to 4 minutes per side.

Transfer each fillet to a plate and top each with half the onions. Serve immediately.

Makes 2 servings. Each (1 fillet plus 1/3 cup onions) serving has: 207 calories, 23 g protein, 4 g carbohydrates, 10 g fat, 2 g saturated fat, 62 mg cholesterol, <1 g fiber, 52 mg sodium

"Smoky" Salmon with Cucumber Tomato Salad (page 182)

"smoky" salmon

Hands-on Time: 5 MINUTES •
Hands-off Time: 1 HOUR TO SOAK THE PLANK (GRILL MUST BE PREHEATED TOWARD THE END OF THIS TIME) PLUS 12 MINUTES TO GRILL

Wooden grill planks are becoming easier and easier to find these days. Stores like Target, Bed, Bath & Beyond, Wal-Mart, and K-Mart all carry them. If you can't find them in a store, they are available for purchase online at amazon.com. Just be sure to pay attention to the type of wood the plank is made from—different varieties of wood give the food a different flavor. And make sure you read the instructions enclosed with the planks for proper cleaning and care.

½ teaspoon extra virgin olive oil
2 (4-ounce) skinless salmon fillets
Sea salt and pepper, to taste
1 wooden grill plank (any variety), soaked in water for at least 1 hour

Place the plank on the grill and preheat the grill to medium heat.

Rub the oil evenly over the salmon fillets. Season them evenly with salt and pepper.

Carefully open the grill. If the plank is ready, it should smoke, and it may crackle; if it begins to warp, flip it over and let it settle. Set the salmon fillets side by side on the plank, not touching. Grill for about 6 minutes. Using a spatula, gently loosen the fillets (they may stick slightly) and flip them. Grill them 4 to 6 minutes more, or until the salmon is cooked to your liking. Serve immediately.

Makes 2 servings. Each (1 fillet) serving has: 172 calories, 23 g protein, 0 g carbohydrates, 8 g fat, 1 g saturated fat, 62 mg cholesterol, 0 g fiber, 50 mg sodium

pan "fried" old bay salmon

Hands-on Time: 12 MINUTES • *Hands-off Time:* NONE

Can't find Old Bay Rub? Try this recipe using Old Bay Seasoning (the 30% less sodium variety, if possible) instead of the rub, which has less salt, and a hint of sugar. Just be aware that using Old Bay Seasoning—even the less-sodium variety—will increase the sodium in this dish.

When you're selecting your salmon, always try to buy the thickest fillets possible (fillets closer to the head of the fish, not the tail). The tail is constantly whipping around, "working out," so the meat there tends to be less tender.

I try to use wild salmon as much as possible because it's more natural and because it's lower in fat and calories. But that's often cost-prohibitive, since it's a lot more rare. It's also tougher to find in some parts of the country. Either wild-caught or farm-raised salmon is fine for this recipe, but using farm-raised adds 1.5 grams of fat and 12 calories per ounce.

$1^1/_2$ teaspoons Old Bay Rub

2 (4-ounce) boneless, skinless salmon fillets, (about $3^1/_2$ × $3^1/_2$ inches square and $3/_4$ inch thick)

Olive oil spray

Lemon wedges, optional

Place a small nonstick skillet over medium-high heat. Rub the seasoning evenly over all sides of each fillet. When the pan is hot, lightly mist it with spray and add the salmon fillets. Cook 1 to 2 minutes per side, or until the outsides are just lightly browned. Then turn the heat to medium and continue cooking until pale pink throughout, 2 to 3 minutes per side. Serve immediately with lemon wedges for squeezing, if desired.

Makes 2 servings. Each (1-fillet) serving has: 167 calories, 23 g protein, trace carbohydrates, 7 g fat, 1 g saturated fat, 62 mg cholesterol, 0 g fiber, 260 mg sodium

orange shrimp

You know those rich, saucy Chinese takeout dishes that are so popular, but that a lot of us avoid because we know they're full of sugar, salt, and fat? Well, this recipe tastes just like those bad-for-you dishes, but it's incredibly low-fat and low in sodium. It also packs a ton of flavor, especially when you consider how few ingredients are used.

If you buy shrimp frozen when it's on sale and keep it in your freezer, you'll likely have all of the necessary ingredients on hand the next time you find yourself tempted by Chinese takeout.

Fortunately, this recipe doesn't skimp on sauce—there's plenty. So it's perfect to toss with steamed snow peas, broccoli, or your favorite vegetables, and/or to serve over brown rice. You can even cook the vegetables in the pan along with the shrimp, but just be aware that the flavor of the vegetables could overpower the delicious orange flavor if you do that.

1 tablespoon cornstarch
1 cup 100% orange juice (not from concentrate, preferably no pulp)
1¼ pounds 21–25 count shrimp (preferably easy-peel), peeled and deveined
Salt and pepper, to taste
Olive oil spray
2 teaspoons crushed garlic, divided (I used Dorot Crushed Garlic)

Put the cornstarch in a medium bowl or measuring cup. Whisking constantly, add enough orange juice to the cornstarch to form a paste. Whisk in the remaining juice and continue whisking until the cornstarch is completely dissolved. Set aside.

Season the shrimp with salt and pepper.

Place a large, nonstick skillet over high heat. When hot, lightly mist the pan with the spray and add the shrimp in an even layer along with the garlic. Cook for 1 to 2 minutes per side, or until the shrimp turns pink and is no longer translucent.

Pour the orange juice mixture over the shrimp, gently stirring it until the sauce has thickened, 2 to 3 minutes.

Makes 4 servings. Each (½ cup) serving has: 157 calories, 24 g protein, 10 g carbohydrates, 2 g fat, trace saturated fat, 172 mg cholesterol, trace fiber, 169 mg sodium

buffalo shrimp

Hands-on Time: 10 MINUTES • *Hands-off Time:* 5 MINUTES TO REST

Instead of buffalo wings, I love buffalo shrimp at times. The shrimp is great because it's nice and meaty, yet you don't have to worry about tenderizing it. Plus this dish is lean, but will still satisfy that craving for hot sauce that makes us want buffalo wings in the first place.

Buy easy-peel or peeled shrimp to save time and have the kids help with the peeling, if possible.

1 pound large (21–25 count or 26–30 count) shrimp, peeled (tail-on, if desired) and deveined
1 tablespoon all-purpose flour
$1/4$ teaspoon cayenne
$1/4$ teaspoon garlic powder
Pinch sea salt
Olive oil spray
2 tablespoons light butter
1 tablespoon hot sauce (an all-natural one like Wing Time, not a thin one like Tabasco), plus more if desired

Rinse the shrimp, and then pat them dry with a paper towel to remove excess moisture.

To a large resealable plastic bag add the flour, cayenne, garlic, and salt. Toss to combine. Add the shrimp and toss thoroughly to coat them evenly.

Place a large nonstick skillet over medium-high heat. When hot, lightly mist the pan with spray and add the shrimp in a single layer, working in batches, if necessary. Cook them until they are lightly browned on the outsides and cooked through, 1 to 2 minutes per side. Remove the cooked shrimp to a plate or bowl.

When all of the shrimp are cooked, turn off the burner. Add the butter and hot sauce to the skillet and, using a wooden spoon, stir constantly until the butter is just melted, being careful not to overcook it. Return the shrimp to the pan. Toss to coat them completely with the sauce. Season with additional hot sauce, if desired. Let the shrimp sit for 5 minutes, and then toss them again (the sauce will thicken slightly and stick better after sitting). Serve immediately.

Makes 4 servings. Each (5 to 7 shrimp) serving has: 159 calories, 23 g protein, 3 g carbohydrates, 6 g fat, 2 g saturated fat, 180 mg cholesterol, trace fiber, 245 mg sodium

bruschettarogies

Hands-on Time: 2 MINUTES •
Hands-off Time: TIME TO BOIL WATER PLUS 5 TO 7 MINUTES

I particularly love this dish because of the meld of temperatures—hot dumplings with cool sauce.

If you haven't tried them, pierogies are Polish dumplings that are similar to ravioli, but the "pasta" is made from flour and potato instead of just flour. Numerous brands of pierogies are available these days, so they're relatively easy to find. Just be sure to read the nutrition information, because while some are very low in fat, others can be quite high. It's sometimes even possible to find whole-wheat, all-natural pierogies. Living Right Natural Foods makes them, though using the same serving size of these will add about 3.5 grams of fat to each three-pierogie serving. To keep the calories as low as the recipe below, eat three all-natural pierogies instead of the manufacturer's suggested serving size of four.

Be mindful when you're buying bruschetta sauce as well. This is another item where brands vary widely. Though olive oil is good for you, overindulging can definitely counter efforts to be fit, and some brands have an extraordinary amount of olive oil.

3 potato and Cheddar pierogies (2.5 g of fat or less for 3 pierogies; I used Mrs. T's)

2 tablespoons prepared bruschetta topping (2 g of fat or less per 2 tablespoon serving, I used Trader Joe's)

Boil the pierogies according to package directions. Drain them and transfer them to a serving bowl. Top with bruschetta. Serve immediately.

Makes 1 serving. 200 calories, 6 g protein, 35 g carbohydrates, 5 g fat, 1 g saturated fat, 5 mg cholesterol, 1 g fiber, 600 mg sodium

136   I CAN'T BELIEVE IT'S NOT FATTENING!

cheddar pierogies with caramelized onions

Hands-on Time: 3 MINUTES (ONIONS MUST BE MADE IN ADVANCE) •
Hands-off Time: TIME TO BOIL WATER PLUS 5 to 7 MINUTES

This is another recipe where caramelized onions work well. Though they're not actually moist, they ensure you're not eating a dry, bland dish. And if you make them ahead (see page 225), you can reheat them in a flash to turn what would otherwise be an ordinary meal into a restaurant-quality one.

3 potato and Cheddar pierogies (2.5 g of fat or less for 3 pierogies; I used Mrs. T's)
1/4 cup Easier-Than-Caramelized Onions (see page 225), reheated if necessary

Boil the pierogies according to package directions. Drain them and transfer them to a serving bowl. Top them with the onions. Serve immediately.

Makes 1 serving. 215 calories, 6 g protein, 37 g carbohydrates, 5 g fat, 1 g saturated fat, 5 mg cholesterol, 2 g fiber, 531 mg sodium

pierogies with kielbasa and sauerkraut

Hands-on Time: 6 MINUTES •
Hands-off Time: TIME TO BOIL WATER PLUS 5 TO 7 MINUTES

My mom recently made this recipe. She called my office and told Stephanie, our "Test Kitchen Goddess," that it should be called Polish Paradise. She was shocked at how quick and easy it was to make, especially for as much as she and my dad loved it.

When spooning the sauerkraut into the measuring cup, it doesn't actually need to be drained, but it shouldn't be accompanied by a lot of excess liquid.

Please note this isn't a dish that should be eaten every night if you're watching your sodium intake, since the amount of sodium is pretty high. That said, the recipe has only a fraction of the sodium it would have if you were to eat something similar in most restaurants.

3 potato and Cheddar pierogies (2.5 g of fat or less for 3 pierogies; I used Mrs. T's)

Olive oil spray

2 ounces smoked turkey sausage or kielbasa (5 g of fat or less per 2-ounce serving), cut into $1/4$-inch-thick rounds on a diagonal (look for it packaged in the refrigerated section, usually near the breakfast meats)

$1/4$ cup sauerkraut from a bag or jar (not canned; look for it in the refrigerated section near the pickles)

Boil the pierogies according to package directions.

Meanwhile, place a small nonstick skillet over medium-high heat. Lightly mist the pan with spray and add the sausage and sauerkraut. Cook for 2 to 4 minutes, or until the sausage is warmed through and begins to brown in spots.

Drain the pierogies and transfer them to a serving bowl. Top them with the sausage and sauerkraut mixture. Serve immediately.

Makes 1 serving. 263 calories, 15 g protein, 38 g carbohydrates, 8 g fat, 2 g saturated fat, 40 mg cholesterol, 2 g fiber, 1,470 mg sodium

pierogies with lemon caper butter

Hands-on Time: 3 MINUTES •
Hands-off Time: TIME TO BOIL WATER PLUS 5 TO 7 MINUTES

Though boxes of pierogies tend to provide many cooking options, my favorite for this dish (and many others) is to boil them. They stay nice and tender, and there's no need to add any fat. The flavor of this dish is subtle, so it's particularly great for those who aren't as in love with spicy foods as I am. Either way, though, it's a great, refreshing recipe for a summer evening.

3 potato and Cheddar pierogies (2.5 g of fat
   or less for 3 pierogies; I used Mrs. T's)
1 teaspoon light butter (from a stick, not tub;
   I used Challenge Light)
1 teaspoon fresh lemon juice
1 teaspoon drained capers
Salt and pepper, to taste

Boil the pierogies according to package directions. Reserve 1 tablespoon of the cooking liquid.

Meanwhile, add the butter and lemon juice to a small nonstick skillet over medium heat. Cook the mixture, stirring frequently, until the butter is just melted. Add the capers and the reserved cooking liquid, and continue heating until the sauce is warm, 1 to 3 minutes. Drain the pierogies and add them to the pan. Gently toss them until they are coated with the sauce. Season with salt and pepper. Serve immediately.

Makes 1 serving. 199 calories, 6 g protein, 35 g carbohydrates, 5 g fat, 2 g saturated fat, 10 mg cholesterol, 1 g fiber, 647 mg sodium

breaded portobello mushrooms
with dijon

Hands-on Time: 5 MINUTES •
Hands-off Time: TIME TO PREHEAT OVEN PLUS 10 TO 14 MINUTES

Lots of folks are tricked by markets that boast to be health food stores or natural food stores or even have the word fresh *in their name. Though there is definitely something to be said for eating foods that are minimally processed, just because you do doesn't mean you'll be healthy in terms of weight, cholesterol, etc.*

I was recently at a natural food market where I saw a breaded portobello mushroom in the deli case. I thought it was a great idea until I looked at the nutritional information. It had a ridiculous amount of total fat, saturated fat, and calories. Believe it or not, the turkey meatballs were almost as bad. So I trudged home and made my own version in minutes. The team in my kitchen was particularly excited about this recipe, especially since each breaded mushroom has only 64 calories!

Olive oil spray (from a spray bottle, not a store-bought, prefilled one that contains propellant; I used a Misto)

1/2 cup (about 14) fat-free herb-seasoned, Caesar, or Italian-seasoned croutons (I used Marie Callender's Fat-Free Herb-Seasoned Croutons)

2 large portobello mushroom caps, rubbed clean with a damp paper towel

4 teaspoons Dijon mustard, divided

Preheat the oven to 400°F. Line a small baking sheet with parchment. Lightly mist the parchment with spray.

Put the croutons in a resealable plastic bag. Using the flat side of a meat mallet or the underside of a skillet, pound the croutons until they are crushed into crumbs, being careful not to crush them too finely (they should be coarser than bread crumbs). Transfer the crumbs to a medium shallow bowl. Set aside.

Brush all sides of one of the mushroom caps with half of the mustard. Dip it in the crumbs to coat it on all sides. Place it on the prepared baking sheet, gills up. Lightly mist the top with spray. Repeat with the remaining mushroom, mustard, and crumbs. Bake the mushrooms until they are cooked through and the breading is crisp, 5 to 7 minutes per side. Serve immediately.

Makes 2 servings. Each (1 breaded mushroom) serving has: 64 calories, 3 g protein, 10 g carbohydrates, trace fat, 0 g saturated fat, 0 mg cholesterol, 1 g fiber, 229 mg sodium

penne and asparagus
with ricotta cheese

Hands-on Time: 8 MINUTES •
Hands-off Time: TIME FOR WATER TO BOIL PLUS 8 TO 10 MINUTES

If you prefer, you can always substitute a brown rice, whole-wheat, or whole-grain pasta for the fiber-enriched variety. I get a lot of letters and e-mails from home cooks around the country saying they are able to make my recipes for the whole family even though their spouses and children won't generally eat healthy food, because my recipes actually taste fattening. To keep with that tradition, I opt for the fiber-enriched pasta since it adds needed fiber to our diets while still tasting more like traditional pasta.

1 (14^1/2-ounce) box of fiber-enriched penne pasta (I used Ronzoni Smart Taste Penne Rigate)

1 pound trimmed asparagus, cut into 2-inch diagonal pieces

2 teaspoons freshly minced garlic

1 cup low-fat ricotta cheese (I used Precious, which is the same as Sorrento in various parts of the country)

1 tablespoon extra virgin olive oil

^{1}/4 cup reduced-fat grated Parmesan cheese (look for it in a plastic canister or jar, not in the refrigerated section)

Sea salt and freshly ground black pepper, to taste

Crushed red pepper flakes, to taste, optional

Cook the pasta according to package directions, omitting any oil or butter.

Two to four minutes before the pasta is done, add the asparagus to the water (2 minutes for thin spears, 4 minutes for thick). Before draining, reserve about 1 cup of the pasta water in a small bowl. Drain the pasta.

Meanwhile, add the garlic, ricotta, and olive oil to a large serving bowl. As soon as the pasta is drained, mix in ^{1}/3 cup of the reserved pasta water. Immediately add the pasta and asparagus and gently toss until the pasta and asparagus are coated with the cheese mixture. Season with salt and pepper. Gently toss again. If the mixture seems too dry, add more reserved pasta water, about ^{1}/4 cup at a time, until no longer dry. Sprinkle the Parmesan over the pasta and sprinkle with the red pepper flakes, if desired. Serve immediately.

Makes 6 servings. Each (about 2-cup) serving has: 318 calories, 15 g protein, 60 g carbohydrates, 7 g fat, 2 g saturated fat, 18 mg cholesterol, 9 g fiber, 183 mg sodium

Ravio-Sagne with Arugula Appetizer Salad (page 184)

ravio-sagne

Hands-on Time: 10 MINUTES •
Hands-off Time: 50 MINUTES PLUS 10 MINUTES TO STAND

This dish is insanely great for potlucks. Instead of other lasagnes that you can slave over for hours, you can now spend just 10 minutes throwing this together. And the best news is that it can be assembled up to 1 day in advance. After preparing it, simply cover it with plastic wrap and store it in the refrigerator (be sure to remove the plastic wrap before baking!) so it can be baked just before serving.

Make sure you find a brand of ravioli with as little fat as possible. Some are laden with tons of fat and calories, yet they don't taste any better than those that are lower in fat and calories. Rosetto also makes a whole-wheat ravioli that's delicious and just as low in fat and calories but packs 6 grams of fiber per serving (I buy it at Whole Foods). Though the bag is slightly smaller (22 ounces instead of 25), so you'll need a bag plus a few more ravioli to make the recipe as written, it's worth buying.

2 cups low-fat, preferably lower-sodium marinara sauce

25-ounce package frozen rectangle cheese ravioli (about 1 inch by 1^1/2 inches; no more than 4 g of fat per 9-piece serving; I used Rosetto)

6 ounces (about 2 cups plus 2 tablespoons) reduced-fat, finely shredded mozzarella cheese (no more than 3 g of fat per ounce; I used Lucerne, found at Safeway chains), divided

^{1}/3 cup finely slivered basil leaves, divided

Preheat the oven to 400°F.

Spoon ^{1}/2 cup sauce evenly into the bottom of an 11 × 7-inch ceramic or glass baking dish. Lay one-third of the ravioli (about 18 pieces) side by side in a single layer to cover the bottom of the dish. Spoon another ^{1}/2 cup sauce evenly over top. Sprinkle one-third of the cheese and one-third of the basil evenly over that. Repeat the layering 2 more times beginning with the ravioli. Cover the dish with foil. Bake for 40 minutes. Remove the foil and continue baking an additional 10 minutes, or until the pasta is heated through and the cheese is melted. Let stand 10 minutes, and then slice into 6 equal pieces and serve immediately.

Makes 6 servings. Each (^{1}/6 casserole) serving has: 301 calories, 18 g protein, 43 g carbohydrates, 7 g fat, 3 g saturated, 26 mg cholesterol, 4 g fiber, 689 mg sodium

tuscan pizza

Hands-on-Time: 5 MINUTES •
Hands-off Time: TIME TO PREHEAT OVEN PLUS 8 TO 10 MINUTES
PLUS 5 MINUTES TO STAND

I love olives. If they had no calories, I would eat them by the bucket. Again, though, they are another ingredient that when eaten in moderation provides good fats our bodies do need. Here, I've used them to make pizza, another of my favorite foods. This throw-together meal will take significantly less time than waiting for takeout. And it's especially great because you can stock the ingredients in your kitchen for that night when you just don't have time to cook.

1 (10-ounce) Boboli whole-wheat pizza crust

2/3 cup low-fat pizza or marinara sauce (lower-sodium, if possible)

3 ounces (about 1 cup) finely shredded reduced-fat mozzarella cheese (no more than 3 g of fat per ounce; I used Lucerne, found at Safeway chains)

7 pitted Kalamata olives, sliced crosswise

5 green Spanish olives (sometimes called Manzanillas), sliced crosswise

2 teaspoons drained capers

1/8 to 1/2 teaspoon crushed red pepper flakes, or more to taste

Preheat the oven to 450°F.

Place the crust on a baking sheet large enough for it to lie flat. Spread the sauce evenly over the crust to cover all but the outer 1/2 inch. Sprinkle the cheese evenly over the sauce, followed by the Kalamatas, green olives, capers, and red pepper flakes. Bake the pizza until the cheese melts and the crust is lightly crisped, 8 to 10 minutes. Let it stand 5 minutes, and then cut it into 8 slices and serve immediately.

Makes 4 servings. Each (2-slice) serving has: 268 calories, 15 g protein, 39 g carbohydrates, 8 g fat, 3 g saturated fat, 8 mg cholesterol, 7 g fiber, 897 mg sodium

chicken parmesan pizza

Hands-on Time: 10 MINUTES •
Hands-off Time: 10 TO 12 MINUTES PLUS 5 MINUTES TO STAND

You can buy pregrilled chicken in grocery stores these days for convenience, or you can make it yourself in bulk a couple of days a week (see Basic Grilled Chicken, page 219). If you make it yourself, you're apt to save a lot of sodium—and likely a lot of money too.

I love adding chicken to pizza. The addition of plenty of lean protein can transform pizza into a very well-balanced meal. Because chicken is so low in fat, it's best to put it under the cheese (instead of on top, like you traditionally would with meat toppings) when making pizza—you'll keep the chicken from drying out.

1 (10-ounce) Boboli whole-wheat pizza crust
3/4 cup low-fat pizza or marinara sauce
   (lower-sodium, if possible)
8 ounces Basic Grilled Chicken (see page
   219) or lean, store-bought grilled chicken,
   cut into bite-sized pieces
2 ounces (about 1/2 cup plus 2 tablespoons)
   finely shredded reduced-fat mozzarella
   cheese (no more than 3 g of fat per
   ounce; I used Lucerne, found at Safeway
   chains)
1 tablespoon grated reduced-fat Parmesan
   cheese (look for it in a plastic canister or
   jar, not in the refrigerated section)
1 to 2 tablespoons fresh basil slivers, optional
1/8 to 1/4 teaspoon crushed red pepper flakes,
   or more to taste, optional

Preheat the oven to 450°F.

Place the crust on a baking sheet large enough for it to lie flat. Spread the sauce evenly over the crust to cover all but the outer 1/2 inch. Top it evenly with the chicken and then the mozzarella, Parmesan, basil, and red pepper flakes, if using. Bake the pizza until the cheese melts and the dough is lightly crisped, 10 to 12 minutes. Transfer it to a platter or cutting board. Let stand 5 minutes, and then slice into 8 equal slices and serve immediately.

Makes 4 servings. Each (2 slice) serving has: 310 calories, 26 g protein, 40 g carbohydrates, 7 g fat, 3 g saturated fat, 39 mg cholesterol, 6 g fiber, 667 mg sodium

grilled chicken, goat cheese, & roasted red pepper pizza

Hands-on Time: 8 MINUTES •
Hands-off Time: 10 TO 12 MINUTES PLUS 5 MINUTES TO STAND

It's best to buy goat cheese that is precrumbled. This will save you time and make it easier to spread the cheese across the entire pizza, requiring less to get some in every bite. If you do buy it in a tube (it may make sense if it's significantly less expensive that way), freeze it slightly before attempting to crumble it. It will crumble much easier.

1 (10-ounce) Boboli whole-wheat pizza crust
1/2 cup low-fat pizza or marinara sauce
  (lower-sodium, if possible)
8 ounces Basic Grilled Chicken (see page
  219) or lean, store-bought grilled chicken,
  cut into 1/2-inch pieces
2/3 cup drained jarred roasted red bell
  pepper strips
2 ounces (about 1/2 cup) goat cheese
  crumbles
Chopped fresh cilantro or basil leaves, to
  taste

Preheat the oven to 450°F.

Place the crust on a baking sheet large enough for it to lie flat. Spread the sauce evenly over the crust to cover all but the outer 1/2 inch. Top the sauce evenly with the chicken, bell pepper strips, and then the goat cheese. Bake until the cheese melts and the crust is lightly crisped, 10 to 12 minutes. Top the pizza with cilantro or basil, and then let it stand 5 minutes. Slice it into 8 equal wedges and serve immediately.

Makes 4 servings. Each (2 slice) serving has: 324 calories, 25 g protein, 40 g carbohydrates, 8 g fat, 4 g saturated fat, 39 mg cholesterol, 6 g fiber, 700 mg sodium

salad pizza with grilled chicken

Hands-on Time: 12 MINUTES • *Hands-off Time:* TIME TO PREHEAT OVEN

I think this might be the most guilt-free pizza I eat. Not only are you getting the health benefits of whole wheat from the tortilla, in addition, nutritious salad greens are included, along with plenty of lean protein.

If you can't find the garlic blend, you can use a garlic spread. Just be sure you find one without too much fat. That said, since you're using only a teaspoon, even one with a bit of fat won't hurt. Just be sure not to use the leftovers of a more fattening one in bulk in another recipe.

1 (about 8-inch-diameter) reduced-fat, whole-wheat flour tortilla (not a low-carb one)

1 teaspoon Gourmet Garden Garlic Blend or frozen garlic (look for Gourmet Garden in a tube in the produce section, or look for frozen garlic at Trader Joe's)

1 ½ teaspoons reduced-fat grated Parmesan cheese (look for it in a plastic canister or jar, not in the refrigerated section)

3 cups (about 3 small handfuls) mixed baby greens

3 tablespoons seeded and finely chopped tomato

1 tablespoon finely chopped red onion

1 tablespoon bottled reduced-fat balsamic or Italian vinaigrette (one with no more than 2 g of fat per tablespoon; I used Newman's Own Light Balsamic Vinaigrette)

4 ounces Basic Grilled Chicken (see page 219) or lean store-bought grilled chicken breast, sliced into strips on the diagonal

Freshly ground black pepper, to taste

Preheat the oven to 400°F.

Place the tortilla on a nonstick baking sheet. Bake it for 3 to 4 minutes. Flip the tortilla and spread the garlic spread evenly over the top, and then sprinkle it evenly with the Parmesan. Bake it another 3 to 5 minutes, or until the tortilla is crisp and lightly browned in spots.

Meanwhile, in a medium glass or plastic mixing bowl, toss the greens, tomato, onion, and vinaigrette.

Transfer the tortilla to a serving plate. Mound the salad atop the crisped tortilla and top it with the chicken. Season with pepper and serve immediately.

Makes 1 serving. 335 calories, 31 g protein, 36 g carbohydrates, 7 g fat, <1 g saturated fat, 65 mg cholesterol, 6 g fiber, 804 mg sodium

ravioli soup

Hands-on Time: 5 MINUTES •
Hands-off Time: TIME TO BOIL BROTH PLUS 5 MINUTES

At first glance, it might seem strange to see the words ravioli *and* soup *together. But I figure if Jewish folks cut through matzo balls and Chinese folks break apart wontons, we Italians should be able to join in by throwing ravioli in our soup.*

Though I'd like to pretend I'm a trendsetter, I've really just created a twist on tortellini soup for the sake of saving fat and calories. In my grocery stores I can find lower-fat ravioli, but I can't find lower-fat tortellini. If you do find the tortellini, feel free to return to the more traditional and make this soup with tortellini. But I'm pretty happy with it as is, and I think you will be too.

Note that if you can find it, Rosetto also makes a whole-wheat ravioli that's delicious and just as low in fat and calories but packs 6 grams of fiber per serving (I buy it at Whole Foods). The bag is slightly smaller (22 ounces instead of 25), so you'd need a bag plus a few more ravioli to make the recipe as written, but it's worth buying.

2 (32-ounce) boxes (or the equivalent) of fat-free, lower-sodium chicken or vegetable broth (not low sodium)

2 medium garlic cloves, smashed with the side of a knife

Freshly ground black pepper, to taste

1 (25-ounce) bag of frozen (or the equivalent) cheese ravioli (about 1 inch by 1 1/2 inches; no more than 4 g of fat per 9-piece serving; I used Rosetto)

8 teaspoons finely chopped flat-leaf parsley leaves

8 teaspoons reduced-fat, grated Parmesan cheese (look for it in a plastic canister or jar, not in the refrigerated section)

Pour the broth into a large stockpot with a lid and place it over high heat. Add the garlic cloves and season the broth with pepper. Cover the pot and bring the liquid to a rolling boil. Using a mesh strainer (with a handle) or a slotted spoon, remove the garlic cloves. Add the ravioli and cook for 5 minutes, or until they are al dente.

Divide the broth and ravioli evenly among 8 serving bowls. Sprinkle 1 teaspoon parsley and 1 teaspoon Parmesan cheese over the top of each bowl. Season with additional pepper, if desired. Serve immediately.

Makes 8 servings. Each (6 to 7 ravioli plus 1 scant cup broth) serving has: 183 calories, 11 g protein, 27 g carbohydrates, 3 g fat, 1 g saturated fat, 13 mg cholesterol, 1 g fiber, 887 mg sodium

Stylin' Steak Fries

Old Bay Potato Wedges

Buffalo Mashed Potatoes

Potato Smashers

Super-Speedy Sweet Potatoes

Powerhouse Polenta Fries

Mexican Mac & Cheese

Cheesy Brown Rice

Spicy Orange Rice Noodles

Lemon Caper Spaghetti Squash

Sautéed Cherry Tomatoes

Red & Green Stir-Fry

Balsamic Roasted Asparagus

Cumin & Lime Black Beans

Creamy Mustard Tossed Green Beans

Green Beans with Roasted Red Bell Peppers

Green Beans with Lime

Grilled Asparagus with Goat Cheese Crumbles

Quick Steamed Lemon Asparagus

Snow Peas with Mint & Pine Nuts

Italian Herbed Zucchini

Steakhouse Mushrooms

Mexican Caprese Salad

Today's Taco Salad

Cucumber Tomato Salad

Chicken Caesar Salad with Sun-Dried Tomatoes

Arugula Appetizer Salad

slimming sides & salads

stylin' steak fries

Hands-on Time: 4 MINUTES •
Hands-off Time: TIME TO PREHEAT OVEN PLUS 25 TO 30 MINUTES

Potatoes have gotten a bad rap in recent years, but the hype is just that—hype. A 5-ounce potato with skin has only 110 calories and more potassium than a medium banana. It also contains 45 percent of the daily recommended value of vitamin C and is a significant source of dietary fiber. It's the toppings that are the problem, not the potatoes themselves.

If you don't love steak fries as much as I do, feel free to make your fries any size—just be sure to watch them carefully, as the cooking time will vary.

2 medium baking potatoes (about 8 ounces each), cut into steak-fry-sized pieces (about 1 inch thick, $^1/_2$ inch wide, and the length of the potato)
1 teaspoon extra virgin olive oil
$^1/_4$ teaspoon sea salt, or more to taste

For crisper fries, preheat the oven to 450°F; for softer fries, preheat the oven to 400°F. Line a large baking sheet with parchment paper.

In a small mixing bowl, toss the fries with the olive oil and $^1/_4$ teaspoon salt. Place them on the prepared baking sheet in a single layer, not touching. Bake them for 15 minutes, and then flip them and bake an additional 10 to 15 minutes, or until tender on the inside and golden brown on the outside. Serve immediately.

Makes 2 servings. Each serving has: 196 calories, 5 g protein, 40 g carbohydrates, 3 g fat, trace saturated fat, 0 mg cholesterol, 5 g fiber, 214 mg sodium

old bay potato wedges

Hands-on Time: 4 MINUTES •
Hands-off Time: TIME TO PREHEAT OVEN PLUS 30 TO 35 MINUTES

I was at a restaurant while on the road for an appearance when I glanced at a menu and saw "Old Bay Potato Wedges." Though the idea seemed perfect, I knew they'd be fried. So instead of ordering them, I immediately texted Stephanie, my Test Kitchen Goddess, and told her we needed to make them. Within days, we created our version, which makes me way happier and more satisfied than any fried version ever could.

2 medium baking potatoes (about 8 ounces each), scrubbed and towel-dried
1 teaspoon extra virgin olive oil
3/4 teaspoon 30% less sodium Old Bay seasoning
Sea salt, to taste

Preheat the oven to 450°F. Line a large baking sheet with parchment paper.

Cut the potatoes in half lengthwise. Cut each half into 4 wedges, creating 16 wedges total. In a small glass or plastic mixing bowl, toss the wedges with the olive oil and Old Bay. Place them on the baking sheet in a single layer, not touching. Bake them 20 minutes, and then flip them and bake them an additional 10 to 15 minutes, or until they are tender on the inside and golden brown on the outside. Season with salt. Serve immediately.

Makes 2 servings. Each serving has: 196 calories, 5 g protein, 40 g carbohydrates, 3 g fat, trace saturated fat, 0 mg cholesterol, 5 g fiber, 156 mg sodium

buffalo mashed potatoes

Hands-on Time: 4 MINUTES • *Hands-off Time:* 10 MINUTES

Most mashed potatoes are full of butter, cream, and other added fats. But this dish pairs wing sauce with blue cheese, packing tons of flavor and thus eliminating the need for added fats or butter.

1 (24-ounce) package Ore-Ida Steam n' Mash Cut Russet Potatoes

1/2 cup plus 2 tablespoons fat-free milk

1 1/2 tablespoons buffalo wing sauce (try to use a thick, all-natural one, but definitely not a thin one like Tabasco; I used Wing Time Hot Buffalo Wing Sauce)

1/4 cup (about 1 ounce) reduced-fat blue cheese (I used Treasure Cave)

Sea salt and pepper, to taste

Microwave the potatoes according to package directions (do not follow remaining package instructions).

Meanwhile, combine the milk and wing sauce in a small microwave-safe measuring cup or bowl. Once the potatoes are cooked, microwave the milk mixture on high in 15-second intervals, or until the mixture is warm.

Put the cooked potatoes in a large bowl. Using a potato masher or large fork, smash them slightly. Add the milk mixture and the blue cheese and continue to mash the potatoes until they are smooth. Season them with salt and pepper. Serve immediately.

Makes 6 servings. Each (about a heaping 1/2-cup) serving has: 125 calories, 5 g protein, 22 g carbohydrates, 1 g fat, <1 g saturated fat, 3 mg cholesterol, 2 g fiber, 394 mg sodium

potato smashers

Hands-on Time: 4 MINUTES •
Hands-off Time: TIME TO BOIL WATER PLUS 20 TO 25 MINUTES

After The Biggest Loser *Season 6 finale, I went to dinner at a steakhouse with some of the contestants and Alison Sweeney's husband, Dave. We were all, of course, trying to order healthy, but it was definitely a challenge. I wound up getting a grilled chicken breast with salsa and "potato smashers." I was expecting lumpy mashed potatoes. Instead, I was served something similar to this yummy potato . . . only it was doused in more butter than all of us combined had probably eaten in years. But it was so simple, and even tastier with just a small amount of light butter, that I knew I had to include it here.*

4 red-skinned or white boiling potatoes
    (about 6 ounces each), scrubbed
Sea salt, to taste
2 tablespoons light butter, melted, divided
4 teaspoons minced fresh chives, divided
Fresh ground black pepper, to taste

Add the potatoes to a large stockpot. Fill the pot so the water is 1 inch higher than the potatoes and add about 1 teaspoon salt, or to taste. Place the pot over high heat and bring the water to a boil. Cook the potatoes for 20 to 25 minutes, or until they are tender. Drain them well.

Transfer each potato to a serving plate. Press the back of a fork into the top of each potato, smashing it until it flattens slightly (it's okay if the potatoes crumble a bit). Drizzle the butter evenly over the top of the potatoes, about $1/2$ tablespoon on each. Sprinkle the chives evenly among them, about 1 teaspoon on each. Season with salt and pepper. Serve immediately.

Makes 4 servings. Each (1-potato) serving has: 144 calories, 3 g protein, 28 g carbohydrates, 3 g fat, 2 g saturated fat, 8 mg cholesterol, 3 g fiber, 58 mg sodium

super-speedy sweet potatoes

Hands-on Time: 6 TO 8 MINUTES (MICROWAVE) OR 3 MINUTES (OVEN) •
Hands-off Time: NONE (MICROWAVE) OR TIME TO PREHEAT OVEN PLUS
45 TO 60 MINUTES (OVEN)

If you can't find 6-ounce potatoes or don't have them on hand, you can simply use one 12-ounce potato. Add 1 minute to the microwave cook time if the potato isn't tender after the 5 to 6 minutes, or an additional 10 to 15 minutes in the oven, and use all of the butter and brown sugar for the one large potato. A 12-ounce potato will make two servings, so the recommendation is to eat only half.

2 medium sweet potatoes (about 6 ounces each), scrubbed

1 teaspoon light butter, divided (stick, not tub; I used Challenge Light)

4 teaspoons light or dark brown sugar, not packed, divided

Microwave Instructions

Using a fork, poke each potato 5 times on all sides. Place the potatoes in a microwave-safe dish large enough for them to lie side by side. Cover the dish loosely with a paper towel. Microwave on high for 3 minutes. Flip the potatoes, being careful not to burn yourself, and continue microwaving an additional 2 to 3 minutes, or until they are tender through. Cut an opening about 4 inches long in the top of each potato and open it wide enough to spoon $^1/_2$ teaspoon butter and 2 teaspoons brown sugar evenly into the center. Return the dish to the microwave and cook another 15 to 30 seconds, or until the butter and sugar are melted. Mash the butter and sugar mixture into the cooked potato to distribute. Serve immediately.

Oven Instructions

Preheat the oven to 400°F. Using a fork, poke each potato 5 times on all sides. Wrap each potato completely in aluminum foil. Bake them for 40 to 45 minutes, or until the potatoes are tender through. Unwrap the potatoes. Cut an opening about 4 inches long in the top of each potato, and open it wide enough to spoon $^1/_2$ teaspoon butter and 2 teaspoons brown sugar evenly into the center. Rewrap the potatoes and bake them for an additional 2 minutes, or until the butter and sugar are melted. Mash the butter and sugar mixture into the cooked potato to distribute. Serve immediately.

Makes 2 servings. Each serving has: 162 calories, 3 g protein, 36 g carbohydrates, 1 g fat, <1 g saturated fat, 3 mg cholesterol, 5 g fiber, 109 mg sodium

powerhouse polenta fries

Hands-on Time: 5 MINUTES •
Hands-off Time: TIME TO PREHEAT OVEN PLUS 30 TO 35 MINUTES

It may seem odd to figure out how to slice a tube of polenta into fries, but it's actually quite simple. Just follow the directions below, imagining the polenta halves are large potatoes. Then cut the fries as if you're cutting them from potatoes.

Olive oil spray (from a spray bottle, not a store-bought, prefilled one that contains propellant; I used a Misto)

1 (18-ounce) tube prepared polenta (look for it with the pasta or tomato sauce in many major grocery stores or at Trader Joe's)

Sea salt, to taste

Ketchup or low-fat marinara sauce, preferably low-fat and lower-sodium, optional

Preheat the oven to 450°F. Place a large piece of parchment on a large baking sheet and lightly mist it with spray.

Cut the polenta in half crosswise, and then cut each half lengthwise into $^{1}/_{2}$-inch-thick fries. Place the fries on the prepared baking sheet in a single layer so they do not touch. Mist the tops with spray, then lightly sprinkle them evenly with salt.

Bake them for 15 minutes. Carefully flip the fries, then mist the tops with spray and salt them. Continue baking an additional 15 to 20 minutes, or until the fries are lightly crisped and golden brown. Serve immediately with ketchup or marinara sauce, if desired.

Makes 4 servings. Each (heaping $^{1}/_{2}$-cup) serving has: 89 calories, 3 g protein, 19 g carbohydrates, trace fat, 0 g saturated fat, 0 mg cholesterol, 1 g fiber, 388 mg sodium

mexican mac & cheese

Hands-on Time: 3 MINUTES •
Hands-off Time: TIME TO BOIL WATER PLUS 8 TO 9 MINUTES

The key to good mac and cheese is gooey cheese and the perfect creamy sauce. Here, I've simplified things to create this twist on a classic. Instead of thickening cream or milk, I grabbed a natural cheese sauce, then simply added a Mexican cheese blend to give it that must-have gooeyness.

7 ounces (about 2 cups) uncooked fiber-enriched or protein-enriched elbow macaroni (I used Ronzoni Smart Taste)
1/2 cup salsa con queso, all-natural if possible
1 1/2 ounces (about 1/2 cup) shredded reduced-fat Mexican cheese blend (I used Sargento)

In a large nonstick stockpot, cook the macaroni according to package directions. Drain it well, then return it to the pot. Stir in the salsa con queso and cheese until combined (if the cheese doesn't melt right away, place the pot over low heat and stir for 1 minute, or until the cheese is melted). Serve immediately.

Makes 4 servings. Each (about 1-cup) serving has: 243 calories, 9 g protein, 41 g carbohydrates, 7 g fat, 2 g saturated fat, 10 mg cholesterol, 5 g fiber, 324 mg sodium

cheesy brown rice

Hands-on Time: 3 MINUTES • *Hands-off Time:* NONE

Make a big batch of brown rice at the beginning of the week and have it ready for reheating in your refrigerator, or buy precooked brown rice in the freezer section of the grocery store.

Though this likely sounds odd, we much preferred the Laughing Cow Light Gourmet Cheese Bites over the Light Original Swiss Cheese wedges in this recipe. When you compare the packages, you'll see they are similar, but everyone in my test kitchen agreed the squares taste better. So trust us when we say it's worth opening the ten squares instead of using a smaller number of wedges.

1 cup cooked brown rice, preferably short-grain, reheated if necessary

10 Laughing Cow Light Gourmet Cheese Bites (squares)

In a small bowl, stir the cheese squares into the hot rice until well combined. Serve immediately.

Makes 2 servings. Each (about ⅟2-cup) serving has: 138 calories, 5 g protein, 24 g carbohydrates, 2 g fat, 1 g saturated fat, 8 mg cholesterol, 2 g fiber, 251 mg sodium

spicy orange rice noodles

Hands-on Time: 7 to 10 MINUTES • *Hands-off Time:* NONE

The exotic flavor of this dish was really surprising to me, considering it uses only a few very basic ingredients. Just note that the rice noodles do stick together slightly (rice noodles are very starchy so they can be a bit sticky). Adding a touch of olive oil keeps them manageable. Sticky or not, I love them, especially used here in this delicious Asian-inspired dish, reminiscent of those super popular boxed noodles. It's sophisticated enough for guests, yet your kids will love it, too!

Note that though these noodles might seem scary to the novice, they're incredibly easy to work with. Try to keep them as intact as possible when pulling them apart. Pull them the long way, so the noodles stay longer, instead of being broken in half. If you don't have a kitchen scale, just estimate and use about ¼ of a 16-ounce package.

2 cups 100% orange juice (not from concentrate, preferably no pulp)

1 teaspoon chili garlic sauce, or more to taste (chili paste is okay too)

4 ounces uncooked angel hair rice noodles (look for them in the international section of your local grocery store)

1 teaspoon extra virgin olive oil

Sea salt to taste

Bring the orange juice to a boil in a medium nonstick saucepan over high heat. Add the chili garlic sauce and rice noodles. Boil the noodles, stirring occasionally (using a nylon pasta fork, if possible), for 2 to 4 minutes or until they are just soft and almost all of the orange juice is absorbed. Remove the pan from the heat and stir in the olive oil. Allow the noodles to stand for about 2 minutes to cool slightly and to absorb the remaining juice. Season with salt. Serve immediately.

Makes 4 servings. Each (generous ½-cup) serving has: 166 calories, 2 g protein, 37 g carbohydrates, 1 g fat, trace saturated fat, 0 mg cholesterol, 2 g fiber, 24 mg sodium

lemon caper spaghetti squash

Hands-on Time: 10 MINUTES •
Hands-off Time: 10 to 12 MINUTES (MICROWAVE) OR 40 TO 45 MINUTES (OVEN)

It's important to avoid buying spaghetti squash that isn't fully ripe. A spaghetti squash that isn't ready will be extremely difficult to cut in half and won't yield a nice, soft texture when cooked. Look for a squash that is a bright, solid yellow (not pale yellow or white in parts). Once the rind is penetrated with a knife, a ripe squash is fairly easy to cut in half.

Also, be sure you have all the ingredients ready to go once the squash is cooked. You'll want to toss everything together when the squash is still hot.

Olive oil spray
1 medium (2½ to 3 pounds) spaghetti squash
1 teaspoon extra virgin olive oil
1 teaspoon light butter
2 to 3 teaspoons fresh lemon juice
1 tablespoon drained capers, or more to taste
1½ teaspoons finely chopped flat-leaf parsley leaves
Sea salt and fresh ground black pepper, to taste

Microwave Instructions

Carefully cut the squash in half lengthwise across the stem. Using a spoon, scrape out the seeds and the fibrous strings attached to them (be careful not to scrape too much, as the edible flesh of the squash scrapes out easily).

Pour ¼ cup water into a microwave-safe dish and place the squash, cut sides up, in the dish. Cover the dish with a microwave-safe plate or tightly with microwave-safe plastic wrap, cutting a small slit in the plastic wrap to vent.

Cook on high for 10 to 12 minutes, or until the squash is cooked through and tender. Let it stand, covered, for 5 minutes.

Using a fork, carefully (the squash will be hot) remove the strands (flesh) of the squash into a medium glass or plastic serving bowl. Discard the rinds. Add the olive oil, butter, and lemon juice and gently mix the ingredients well to combine. Stir in the capers and parsley. Season with salt and pepper. Serve immediately.

Oven Instructions

Follow the microwave instructions, but instead of microwaving the scraped-out squash halves, bake them as follows: Preheat the oven to 375°F. Then line a medium baking sheet with foil and lightly mist it with spray. Place the halves, cut sides down, on the prepared baking sheet. Bake until tender enough that a knife can be easily inserted into the flesh, 40 to 45 minutes. Flip the halves over so the cut sides are up. Let them cool about 5 minutes.

Makes 4 servings. Each (about 1-cup) serving has: 86 calories, 2 g protein, 16 g carbohydrates, 3 g fat, <1 g saturated fat, 1 mg cholesterol, trace fiber, 110 mg sodium

sautéed cherry tomatoes

Hands-on Time: 7 MINUTES • *Hands-off Time:* NONE

For this recipe, it's best to cut the basil into fine slivers. Though it seems like that might take some time, it doesn't have to. Just stack a few basil leaves, then roll the stack from the stem end to the tip. Then make fine cuts across the miniature "log" of leaves. You'll have a pile of long slivers that create the perfect flavor burst in this recipe and are excellent for garnishing other dishes in seconds.

1 teaspoon extra virgin olive oil
1/2 pound cherry or grape tomatoes
1/4 teaspoon garlic powder
2 teaspoons fresh basil leaf slivers
Sea salt and black pepper, to taste

Place a medium nonstick skillet over medium-high heat. When hot, add the oil, the tomatoes, and the garlic powder. Gently shake the pan to combine the ingredients well. Cook the tomatoes, stirring often, until they are tender and the skins begin to split (it's okay if the skins brown a little), about 5 minutes. Sprinkle the basil over the tomatoes. Season with salt and pepper. Serve immediately.

Makes 2 servings. Each (about 3/4-cup) serving has: 43 calories, 1 g protein, 5 g carbohydrates, 3 g fat, trace saturated fat, 0 mg cholesterol, 1 g fiber, 6 mg sodium

red & green stir-fry

Hands-on Time: 6 MINUTES • *Hands-off Time:* NONE

Snow peas with tomatoes—it may seem an odd combination at first, but everyone in my office was really excited about this dish. Between the crisp peas and juicy tomatoes, it has a great texture and flavor, and it's definitely different from the traditional veggie sides we're used to.

1 teaspoon extra virgin olive oil

1 cup snow peas or Chinese peas

1 cup cherry or grape tomatoes

1 teaspoon (about 1 small clove) freshly minced garlic

Sea salt and pepper, to taste

Place a medium nonstick skillet over medium-high heat. When hot, add the olive oil, peas, tomatoes, and garlic. Cook, stirring occasionally, until the peas are crisp-tender and the tomatoes are warmed through, about 3 minutes. Season with salt and pepper. Serve immediately.

Makes 2 servings. Each (scant 1-cup serving) has: 49 calories, 2 g protein, 6 g carbohydrates, 3 g fat, trace saturated fat, 2 g fiber, 5 mg sodium

balsamic roasted asparagus

Hands-on Time: 4 MINUTES •
Hands-off Time: 10 MINUTES TO MARINATE PLUS 7 to 10 MINUTES

Please note the thickness of asparagus spears varies widely. Thinner spears take only a few minutes to cook, while thicker spears easily take 6 minutes or even longer with this preparation. So plan based on the thickness of the spears you have, and make sure to stop cooking them as soon as they reach desired doneness.

1 pound asparagus, trimmed by snapping the thicker ends off where they break naturally (about 10 to 12 ounces after trimming)

1/2 teaspoon extra virgin olive oil

2 teaspoons balsamic vinegar, divided

Sea salt and fresh ground pepper

Preheat the oven to 425°F.

In a large bowl, toss the spears in the oil and 1 teaspoon of the vinegar. Season with salt and pepper. Let the seasoned asparagus sit for 10 minutes.

Lay the spears in a single layer on a medium nonstick baking sheet. Bake them for 4 minutes, flip them, and continue baking until the spears are crisp-tender, 3 to 6 minutes depending on thickness. Drizzle the remaining vinegar over the spears and toss well to coat. Season with salt and pepper to taste. Serve immediately.

Makes 2 servings. Each serving has: 60 calories, 4 g protein, 8 g carbohydrates, 1 g fat, trace saturated fat, 0 mg cholesterol, 4 g fiber, 2 mg sodium

cumin & lime black beans

These beans are a great prepare-ahead option. They reheat well, and the flavor is even better after a couple of hours. Try them chilled with a few baked tortilla chips for an excellent high-fiber snack. Or heat them up—they're fantastic stirred into brown rice for a tasty side dish to accompany Luau London Broil (see page 105). Or simply toss the chilled beans into a salad.

1 (15-ounce) can 50%-less-sodium black beans, drained

1½ tablespoons finely chopped onion (I used red onion, but any variety is okay)

1 tablespoon fresh lime juice

1 tablespoon finely chopped cilantro leaves

¼ teaspoon ground cumin

Sea salt and fresh ground black pepper, to taste

Microwave Instructions

Add the beans to a medium microwave-safe bowl. Cover the bowl with a microwave-safe plate. Microwave the beans on high until they are heated through, about 1 minute.

Stir in the onion, lime juice, cilantro, and cumin until well combined. Season with salt and pepper to taste. Serve immediately, or store in an airtight container in the refrigerator for up to 2 days.

Stovetop Instructions

Instead of microwaving the beans, heat them over medium heat in a small saucepan, stirring occasionally, until warmed, 5 to 7 minutes. Then follow the remaining instructions, mixing them directly in the pan, removed from the heat.

Makes 3 servings. Each (heaping ½-cup) serving has: 82 calories, 6 g protein, 20 g carbohydrates, trace fat, 0 g saturated fat, 0 mg cholesterol, 7 g fiber, 291 mg sodium

creamy mustard tossed green beans

Hands-on Time: 5 MINUTES •
Hands-off Time: TIME TO BOIL WATER PLUS 3 TO 4 MINUTES (STOVETOP) OR
3 TO 5 MINUTES (MICROWAVE)

This simple recipe actually makes quite an elegant side dish. Though the sauce contains only two ingredients, it has a complex flavor. Your guests will think you spent a ton of time, but you can have the dish ready in the few minutes it takes to steam the green beans.

1 pound green beans, trimmed
2 tablespoons stone-ground or whole-grain
     mustard
¼ cup light sour cream
Sea salt and fresh ground black pepper, to
     taste

Meanwhile, mix the mustard and sour cream in a small bowl until well combined.

Transfer the beans to a large glass or plastic serving bowl and add the mustard mixture. Toss well to coat. Season with salt and pepper. Serve immediately.

Stovetop Instructions

Place a steamer insert in a large pot and add enough water to reach just below the insert. Place the pot over high heat, cover with a lid, and bring the water to a boil. Add the green beans and re-cover the pot, leaving the lid slightly ajar. Steam the beans for 3 to 5 minutes, or until they are crisp-tender. Drain them well.

Microwave Instructions

Follow the stovetop directions, except instead of cooking the beans in a steamer, put 3 tablespoons water and the green beans in a medium microwave-safe bowl or dish. Cover the dish with a microwave-safe plate. Microwave on high for 3 to 4 minutes, or until the beans are crisp-tender. Drain them well.

Makes 4 servings. Each (about 1-cup) serving has: 47 calories, 2 g protein, 8 g carbohydrates, 1 g fat, <1 g saturated fat, 5 mg cholesterol, 4 g fiber, 108 mg sodium

green beans with roasted red bell peppers

Hands-on Time: 8 TO 10 MINUTES •
Hands-off Time: TIME TO BOIL WATER PLUS 3 TO 5 MINUTES (STOVETOP) OR
3 TO 4 MINUTES (MICROWAVE)

Green beans are such a versatile vegetable. I love coming up with different flavor combinations for them. They steam quickly, so they are always a great throw-together side dish. I love jarred roasted red peppers for the same reason—they are a flavorful, convenient ingredient to have on hand. So it made sense to combine the two to create this simple and tasty side dish.

Note that, as the recipe is written, these green beans are very crisp, which is how I like them. Feel free to cook them longer if you like softer beans.

1 pound green beans, trimmed
1 teaspoon extra virgin olive oil
1 teaspoon freshly minced garlic
1/2 cup thinly sliced, drained jarred roasted
    red bell pepper strips
Sea salt and pepper, to taste

Stovetop Instructions
Place a steamer insert in a large pot and add enough water to reach just below the insert. Place the pot over high heat, cover with a lid, and bring the water to a boil. Add the green beans and re-cover the pot, leaving the lid slightly ajar. Steam the beans for 3 to 5 minutes, or until they are crisp-tender. Drain them well.

When the beans are almost done, place a large nonstick skillet over medium-high heat. Add the olive oil and garlic and cook for 1 minute, or until the garlic begins to soften. Add the bell peppers, followed by the green beans. Toss the mixture 1 to 2 minutes, or until it is warmed through. Season with salt and pepper. Serve immediately.

Microwave Instructions
Follow the directions above, except instead of cooking the beans in a steamer, add 3 tablespoons water and the green beans to a medium microwave-safe bowl or dish. Cover the dish with a microwave-safe plate. Microwave on high for 3 to 4 minutes, or until the beans are crisp-tender. Drain them well.

Makes 4 servings. Each (1-cup) serving has: 52 calories, 1 g protein, 10 g carbohydrates, 1 g fat, trace saturated fat, 0 mg cholesterol, 4 g fiber, 113 mg sodium

green beans with lime

Hands-on Time: 5 MINUTES •
Hands-off Time: 8 TO 10 MINUTES TO BOIL WATER PLUS 3 TO 5 MINUTES
(STOVETOP) OR 3 TO 4 MINUTES (MICROWAVE)

Have you ever tried using fancy sea salts in your cooking? This recipe is a great place to try a special salt. Because the flavors are so simple, a nice salt really stands out and pairs perfectly with the beans and lime juice. If you happen to have little girls, it's always fun to use pink sea salt that you shave yourself—they're likely to think it looks like a jewel. That said, traditional sea salt tastes great, too.

If you're entertaining with this dish, be sure to toss the beans in the lime juice and salt just before serving your guests. The acid in the lime juice may cause the beans to eventually turn brown (though even if this happens, they'll still taste great).

½ pound green beans, trimmed

2 teaspoons to 1 tablespoon lime juice, or more to taste

Sea salt to taste

Stovetop Instructions

Place a steamer insert in a large pot and add enough water to reach just below the insert. Place the pot over high heat, cover it, and bring the water to a boil. Add the green beans and re-cover the pot, leaving the lid slightly ajar. Steam the beans for 3 to 5 minutes, or until they are crisp-tender. Drain them well.

Transfer the beans to a medium glass or plastic mixing bowl. Toss the beans with the lime juice. Season with salt. Serve immediately.

Microwave Instructions

Follow the directions above, except instead of cooking the beans in a steamer, put 3 tablespoons water and the green beans in a medium microwave-safe bowl or dish. Cover the dish with a microwave-safe plate. Microwave on high for 3 to 4 minutes, or until the beans are crisp-tender. Drain them well. Serve immediately.

Makes 2 servings. Each (about 1-cup) serving has: 29 calories, 1 g protein, 7 g carbohydrates, 0 g fat, 0 g saturated fat, 0 mg cholesterol, 4 g fiber, trace sodium

grilled asparagus with goat cheese crumbles

Hands-on Time: 8 MINUTES • *Hands-off Time:* TIME TO PREHEAT GRILL

I love using goat cheese in my healthy cooking. Although it has 6 grams of fat per ounce, I find I don't need to use nearly as much as I do of other cheeses since it has such a great strong punch of flavor. I've served this asparagus side at many a dinner party, and guests have always raved.

1$\frac{1}{2}$ pounds asparagus, trimmed by snapping the thicker ends off where they break naturally
1 teaspoon extra virgin olive oil
Sea salt and pepper, to taste
1$\frac{1}{2}$ ounces (about $\frac{1}{3}$ cup) goat cheese crumbles

Preheat a grill to high.

In a large bowl, toss the asparagus spears with the oil, salt, and pepper until combined.

Grill the spears in a single layer, rotating them about $\frac{1}{4}$ turn every minute or so until they are crisp-tender, 2 to 5 minutes, depending on thickness. Transfer the spears to a serving platter and top them evenly with the goat cheese. Serve immediately.

Makes 4 servings. Each (about 1-cup) serving has: 69 calories, 4 g protein, 5 g carbohydrates, 3 g fat, 2 g saturated fat, 5 mg cholesterol, 2 g fiber, 39 mg sodium

quick steamed lemon asparagus

Hands-on Time: 7 MINUTES •
Hands-off Time: TIME TO BOIL WATER PLUS 3 TO 5 MINUTES (STOVETOP) OR
2 TO 4 MINUTES (MICROWAVE)

Asparagus tends to be expensive when it's not in season and is ridiculously affordable when it is. Though it's usually available year round, the best time to seek asparagus is from February through June, with April being the prime month. During the peak of asparagus season, I've seen it for as little as 97 cents per pound even in Los Angeles and New York City, where grocery prices are far from ideal.

Be sure to chop the garlic very finely (aka: mince) in this recipe in order to achieve the perfect balance. If it's too coarse you may find the garlic to be overpowering.

1 pound asparagus, trimmed by snapping off the thicker ends where they break naturally

1 teaspoon extra virgin olive oil

2 teaspoons freshly minced garlic

2 teaspoons fresh lemon juice

1/8 teaspoon crushed red pepper flakes, or more to taste

Sea salt, to taste

Stovetop Instructions

Place a steamer insert in a large nonstick pot. Fill the pot with enough water to reach just below the insert. Cover the pot and place it over high heat. Bring the water to a boil. Add the asparagus, re-cover the pot (leaving the lid slightly ajar), and steam until crisp-tender, 3 to 5 minutes. Empty the pot into a strainer.

Return the pot to the stove over medium-high heat. Add the olive oil, garlic, and lemon juice. Cook the mixture, stirring occasionally, until the garlic begins to soften, 1 to 2 minutes. Remove the pot from the heat and gently toss the well-drained spears in the garlic mixture until they are coated. Add the pepper flakes and season with salt. Serve immediately.

Microwave Instructions

Toss the asparagus with the olive oil, garlic, lemon juice, and 2 teaspoons water in a large microwave-safe bowl or dish. Cover the bowl or dish with a microwave-safe plate. Microwave on high until the spears are tender, 2 to 4 minutes. Add the pepper flakes and season with salt. Serve immediately.

Makes 2 generous servings. Each serving has: 72 calories, 4 g protein, 9 g carbohydrates, 2 g fat, trace saturated fat, 0 mg cholesterol, 4 g fiber, <1 mg sodium

snow peas with mint and pine nuts

Hands-on Time: 9 MINUTES • *Hands-off Time:* NONE

As with other nuts, you may find a variety of pine nuts available in your local grocery store. Toasted, salted, dry-roasted, raw, and even seasoned varieties are available in markets today. Be sure to look for pine nuts that are raw or dry-roasted, which means they've been roasted without any added oils or fats. Though I normally prefer dry-roasted, here they'll toast in the pan, which will give the dish great flavor.

To trim peas, just break off the stem end and strip the string away from the edge. It's a great project for the kids.

¼ teaspoon olive oil
½ pound snow peas or Chinese peas,
    trimmed and strings removed
1 tablespoon dry-roasted or raw pine nuts
    (sometimes called *pignoli*)
1 teaspoon freshly minced garlic
¼ teaspoon toasted or roasted sesame oil
1 teaspoon chopped fresh mint leaves
Sea salt, to taste

Place a large nonstick skillet over medium-high heat. Add the olive oil, peas, pine nuts, and garlic. Cook them, stirring occasionally, until the snow peas are crisp-tender, 2 to 3 minutes (do not overcook them or they will get mushy). Remove the pan from the heat. Stir in the sesame oil and mint. Season with salt. Serve immediately.

Makes 2 generous servings. Each (heaping 1-cup) serving has: 95 calories, 3 g protein, 10 g carbohydrates, 4 g fat, trace saturated fat, 0 mg cholesterol, 3 g fiber, 14 mg sodium

italian herbed zucchini

Hands-on Time: 9 MINUTES • *Hands-off Time:* NONE

This dish has few ingredients but a complex flavor. I love using Gourmet Garden's Italian Seasoning Herb Blend here because you can really taste all of the individual herbs without going to the trouble of washing, drying, and chopping them. If you find another brand, that will work too. We've found Gourmet Garden is most common across the country. Though it seems pricy at first, it's really not if you consider how many uses you'll get from one tube and how long it lasts (be sure to check the date when you buy it to get one that will last for months).

½ teaspoon olive oil
½ pound trimmed fresh zucchini, cut into
    ¼-inch rounds
1 teaspoon freshly minced garlic
1 teaspoon Gourmet Garden Italian
    Seasoning Herb Blend (look for it in
    tubes in the produce section or online at
    gourmetgarden.com)
Sea salt and pepper, to taste

Place a large nonstick skillet over medium-high heat. Add the olive oil, zucchini, garlic, and herb blend to the pan. Cook the zucchini, stirring occasionally, until it's tender and begins to brown in spots, 4 to 6 minutes. Season with salt and pepper. Serve immediately.

Makes 2 servings. Each (½-cup) serving has: 37 calories, 1 g protein, 5 g carbohydrates, 1 g fat, trace saturated fat, 0 mg cholesterol, 1 g fiber, 78 mg sodium

steakhouse mushrooms

You'll notice the cooking time of the mushrooms may be as short as 5 minutes or as long as 10 minutes, depending on the thickness of the sliced mushrooms you buy. If your mushrooms are thinner, they'll take less time. Thicker slices will obviously take a bit longer. However, thick or thin, this recipe will cooperate nicely. Just make sure to pay attention to the cooking time.

1 teaspoon extra virgin olive oil
1 pound sliced button mushrooms
1 tablespoon freshly minced garlic
2 tablespoons steak sauce (I used A-1)
Sea salt and pepper, to taste

Preheat a large nonstick skillet over medium-high heat. Add the olive oil, mushrooms, and garlic. Cook them, stirring occasionally, until the mushrooms become tender, 3 to 5 minutes. Add the steak sauce and continue cooking the mixture for 5 to 8 minutes, or until the mushrooms begin to brown. Season with salt and pepper. Serve immediately.

Makes 4 servings. Each (about-1/2 cup) serving has: 46 calories, 4 g protein, 6 g carbohydrates, 2 g fat, trace saturated fat, 0 mg cholesterol, 1 g fiber, 146 mg sodium

mexican caprese salad

Hands-on Time: 5 MINUTES • *Hands-off Time:* NONE

When using fresh herbs, be sure to dry them thoroughly after washing them so they are fluffy, not dense, when chopped. You not only get a more precise measurement, but they'll also distribute more evenly in your dishes.

2 medium plum tomatoes, stemmed and cut into $^1/_4$-inch-thick slices

Olive oil spray (from a spray bottle, not a store-bought, prefilled one that contains propellant; I used a Misto)

1 small lime wedge

Sea salt and pepper, to taste

1 ounce finely crumbled queso fresco (look for it in the refrigerated section with other international ingredients)

1$^1/_2$ teaspoons chopped cilantro leaves, or more to taste

Place one of the tomato slices in the center of a large dinner plate. Arrange the remaining slices, overlapping slightly, forming rings around the center slice until all the tomatoes are used. Lightly mist the tomatoes with spray. Squeeze the lime wedge evenly over the tomato slices. Season with salt and pepper. Then, leaving the outer diameter of the tomato slices bare, sprinkle the cheese and then the cilantro over the top. Serve immediately.

Makes 1 serving. 66 calories, 5 g protein, 6 g carbohydrates, 3 g fat, 2 g saturated fat, 9 mg cholesterol, 2 g fiber, 44 mg sodium

today's taco salad

Hands-on Time: 10 MINUTES • *Hands-off Time:* NONE

When making salads at home, make sure your lettuce is well dried. Here, also be sure the salsa or pico de gallo is completely drained of extra moisture by quickly throwing it in a fine sieve and then gently pressing it with a spoon. Eliminating moisture from the ingredients ensures the finished salad isn't watery. Well-dried ingredients yield a restaurant-quality (or better!) salad.

To make this dish even more special, add low-fat cheese or fresh cilantro.

4 ounces 96% lean ground beef

1/2 to 1 teaspoon salt-free Mexican seasoning or rub (I used Southwest Chipotle Mrs. Dash)

Salt, to taste, optional

3 cups finely chopped arugula or romaine, or a combination

2/3 cup well-drained fresh pico de gallo or salsa

1/2 ounce baked tortilla chips, crushed with your hands

2 tablespoons low-fat Mexican ranch or ranch dressing (I used Follow Your Heart's Spicy Southwest Ranch)

Preheat a small nonstick skillet over medium-high heat. When hot, add the beef, seasoning or rub, and salt. Cook the beef, breaking it into large chunks with a wooden spoon, until no longer pink, 2 to 4 minutes. Let the beef cool at least 1 minute before adding it to the salad.

Meanwhile, place the greens, pico de gallo, and chips in a large glass or plastic mixing bowl. Drizzle the dressing over the top, add the beef, and toss well. Serve immediately.

Makes 1 salad (3½ cups). 257 calories, 26 g protein, 24 g carbohydrates, 8 g fat, 2 g saturated fat, 60 mg cholesterol, 2 g fiber, 396 mg sodium

cucumber tomato salad

Hands-on Time: 4 MINUTES • *Hands-off Time:* NONE

Though I love traditional salads, I'm a big fan of salads that don't include lettuce, especially in summer months when it's warm. There's something about a bowl of fresh, crisp veggies spiked with a bit of cheese that I find satisfying. And it doesn't hurt that they provide fiber and fill you up with so few calories. Here's one variation I make often.

1 cup ½-inch cubes English or seeded
    cucumber
1 cup halved cherry tomatoes
⅓ cup small red onion slivers
2 teaspoons light balsamic vinaigrette (no
    more than 2 g of fat per tablespoon; I
    used Newman's Own Light Balsamic
    Vinaigrette)
1 teaspoon balsamic vinegar, plus more to
    taste, if desired
½ ounce (2 tablespoons) goat cheese
    crumbles
Sea salt and pepper, to taste

Toss the cucumber, tomatoes, and onion with the vinaigrette and vinegar in a medium mixing bowl. Add the goat cheese, salt, and pepper, and toss gently to combine. Serve immediately.

Makes 2 servings. Each (about heaping 1-cup) serving has: 57 calories, 3 g protein, 7 g carbohydrates, 2 g fat, 1 g saturated fat, 3 mg cholesterol, 1 g fiber, 111 mg sodium

chicken caesar salad with sun-dried tomatoes

Hands-on Time: 4 MINUTES • *Hands-off Time:* NONE

Depending on the flavor and thickness of the brand of dressing you buy, you may want to consider adding a little lemon juice to it before tossing it with the salad. Lemon can really brighten the flavor and/or thin thicker dressings (thus requiring less dressing). Be careful, though—some brands are already pretty acidic, so adding lemon juice may make the dressing sour.
Buy prewashed lettuces to save time.

3 cups bagged romaine

4 ounces Basic Grilled Chicken (see page 219) or lean store-bought grilled chicken breast strips

1/2 ounce (scant 1/4 cup) sun-dried tomato strips, or about 6 rehydrated sun-dried tomato halves (not oil-packed), cut into strips

10 fat-free herb-seasoned croutons (I used Marie Callender's Fat-Free Herb Seasoned Croutons)

2 tablespoons bottled light creamy Caesar salad dressing (one that has 8 g of fat or less per 2-tablespoon serving; I used Ken's Steakhouse Light Creamy Caesar)

1 teaspoon reduced-fat grated Parmesan cheese (look for it in a plastic canister or jar, not in the refrigerated section)

Freshly ground black pepper, to taste, optional

Toss the lettuce, chicken, sun-dried tomatoes, croutons, and dressing in a large glass or plastic mixing bowl until well combined. Top with Parmesan and pepper, if desired. Serve immediately.

Makes 1 (3½-cup) serving. 343 calories, 32 g protein, 27 g carbohydrates, 11 g fat, 2 g saturated fat, 70 mg cholesterol, 3 g fiber, 892 mg sodium

arugula appetizer salad

Hands-on Time: 4 MINUTES • *Hands-off Time:* NONE

I am pretty limited in the veggies I love, so I find myself eating the same ones often. Many years ago, I went to a restaurant in Beverly Hills, and they had an arugula salad. I'd never had arugula, but I was feeling adventurous. Ever since, arugula has been my favorite salad green—in part because I love it, but also because it's one of the darker greens and thus has more nutrients than iceberg. Now I admit it's a bit bitter and may not be everyone's favorite. But I'd definitely recommend giving arugula a try. If you like it half as much as I do, you'll love this simple salad.

3 cups (about 3 large handfuls) loosely
    packed prewashed arugula leaves
1/3 cup cherry or grape tomatoes
1 tablespoon light balsamic vinaigrette
    (no more than 2 g fat per tablespoon;
    I used Newman's Own Light Balsamic
    Vinaigrette)
1/4 ounce shaved Parmesan or Romano
    cheese
Freshly ground black pepper, to taste,
    optional

In a medium glass or plastic mixing bowl, toss the arugula, tomatoes, and vinaigrette. Top with the cheese. Season with black pepper, if desired. Serve immediately.

Makes 1 (3-cup) serving. 71 calories, 4 g protein, 5 g carbohydrates, 4 g fat, 1 g saturated fat, 5 mg cholesterol, 2 g fiber, 351 mg sodium

decadent desserts & sweet snacks

peppermint brownie "pizza"

Hands-on Time: 8 MINUTES •
Hands-off Time: TIME TO PREHEAT OVEN PLUS 17 TO 19 MINUTES
PLUS 25 TO 30 MINUTES COOLING TIME

Ever since I created my Chocolate Chocolate Brownie cups, which are an even easier version of my brownies that Jenna Fischer from The Office *raved about on* The Tonight Show with Jay Leno, *saying, "They played no small part in my recovery [speaking of her back injury]," I've been particular about eating only a select few varieties of brownies. Because mine taste like they are full of fat, I don't see a reason to eat actual fatty ones that don't taste any better. I will say, however, that when prepared as suggested as part of this recipe, the No Pudge! Brownies are definitely worth the calories. This recipe even shocked my team—it's truly delicious, not to mention fun!*

To crush the peppermints, place the unwrapped candies in a resealable zip-top bag. Using the flat end of a meat mallet or the bottom of a heavy skillet, pound them until they are crushed into fine shavings. If you really want to save time, look for peppermint sprinkles near ice cream cones and ice cream toppings (brands such as Ken Craft and Wilton make them). They're more expensive than buying the peppermints and crushing them yourself, but they're a timesaver!

If you're not serving this pizza to your guests immediately, add the toppings to the brownie just before serving. If made too far ahead, the peppermints tend to run slightly on the whipped topping so it won't look quite as pretty (though it will still taste delicious!).

Butter-flavored cooking spray

2/3 cup Fiber One or naturally sweetened fat-free vanilla yogurt

1 box (13.7 ounces) No Pudge! Original Fudge Brownie Mix (look for it in the baking or natural foods aisle in your grocery store or at Trader Joe's)

1 cup fat-free frozen whipped topping, defrosted

2 tablespoons finely crushed peppermint disks or candy canes

1 tablespoon chocolate syrup

Preheat the oven to 350°F. Mist a 10½-inch tart pan with spray (as a backup, you can use a 10-inch nonstick deep-dish pizza pan, but the brownie won't pop out as easily as from a tart pan).

In a medium bowl, stir the yogurt into the brownie mix until well combined. Pour the mixture into the prepared pan and spread it with a spatula so it evenly covers the bottom of the pan. Bake for 17 to 19 minutes, or until a toothpick inserted in the center is no longer wet (a few crumbs are okay). *(continued)*

Allow the brownie to cool completely. Spoon the whipped topping into the center and then, using a spatula, spread it to evenly cover all but the outer $^1/_2$-inch of the brownie. Sprinkle the crushed candies evenly over the top. Drizzle the syrup in a fine stream from the edge of a spoon to create a criss-cross pattern. Cut into 8 equal wedges. Serve immediately, or refrigerate for up to 2 days.

Makes 8 servings. Each serving made with Fiber One yogurt has: 142 calories, 3 g protein, 30 g carbohydrates, trace fat, 0 g saturated fat, <1 mg cholesterol, 2 g fiber, 107 mg sodium; Each serving made with naturally sweetened yogurt has: 145 calories, 3 g protein, 30 g carbohydrates, trace fat, 0 g saturated fat, <1 mg cholesterol, 1 g fiber, 110 mg sodium

chipper chipwich

Hands-on Time: 3 MINUTES • *Hands-off Time:* AT LEAST 1 HOUR TO FREEZE

Make several of these low-fat chipwiches at once and store them in your freezer so you have some on hand for later. For freezing, stick the wrapped sandwiches in resealable freezer bags to keep the ice cream from getting icy.

2 reduced-fat chocolate chip cookies (10 to 12 g per cookie; I used Chips Ahoy! Reduced Fat Real Chocolate Chip Cookies)

2 tablespoons fat-free churned vanilla ice cream (I used Breyer's Double Churn)

Spread the ice cream evenly over the bottom of one of the cookies. Place the other cookie atop the ice cream, smooth side down, to form a sandwich. Wrap the sandwich snugly in plastic wrap and freeze for at least 1 hour, or up to 10 days.

Makes 1 serving. 117 calories, 1 g protein, 21 g carbohydrates, 3 g fat, 1 g saturated fat, 0 mg cholesterol, 1 g fiber, 106 mg sodium

mint fudge brownie sundae

Hands-on Time: 4 MINUTES •
Hands-off Time: 3 TO 5 MINUTES TO COOL (MICROWAVE) OR TIME TO PREHEAT
OVEN PLUS 12 TO 14 MINUTES PLUS 3 TO 5 MINUTES TO COOL (OVEN)

*I don't consider myself a snob at all . . . except maybe when it comes to brownies. I've tasted
very few brownies that are low in fat that I truly love. My favorites are my Chocolate Chocolate Brownie Cups, from* The Most Decadent Diet Ever! *(Broadway, 2008), but I must say
the No Pudge! brownie mix is astoundingly tasty for a boxed product. The brownies and these
sundaes are definitely worth a try.*

2 tablespoons No Pudge! Mint Fudge
   Brownie Mix (look for it in the baking or
   natural foods aisle of your grocery store
   or at Trader Joe's)
1 tablespoon Fiber One or naturally
   sweetened, fat-free vanilla yogurt
1/3 cup fat-free churned vanilla ice cream
   (I used Breyer's Double Churn)
2 teaspoons chocolate syrup
1 tablespoon fat-free aerosol whipped
   topping

Microwave Instructions

Stir the brownie mix and yogurt in a microwave-safe, 3^1/2-inch-diameter ramekin or glass
bowl until well combined. Scrape the sides of
the bowl or ramekin, pushing the batter to the
bottom. Microwave on high for 45 seconds to
1 minute, or until a toothpick inserted in the
center comes out dry (a few crumbs are okay).
Allow the brownie to cool for 3 to 5 minutes.
Top the cooked brownie with the ice cream,
followed by the chocolate sauce and whipped
topping. Serve immediately.

Oven Instructions

Follow the microwave instructions, except instead of microwaving the brownie, bake it in a
preheated 350°F oven (in the ramekin) for 12
to 14 minutes, or until cooked through.

Makes 1 sundae. Made with Fiber One yogurt: 233 calories, 5 g protein, 53 g carbohydrates,
0 g fat, 0 g saturated fat, <1 mg cholesterol, 4 g fiber, 173 mg sodium; made with naturally
sweetened yogurt: 234 calories, 5 g protein, 53 g carbohydrates, 0 g fat, 0 g saturated fat, trace
cholesterol, 3 g fiber, 175 mg sodium

kick-butt kahlùa sundae

Hands-on Time: 3 MINUTES • *Hands-off Time:* NONE

When I was a child, I don't think I ever saw my mother drink unless we were on the occasional vacation and she ordered a piña colada. I do, however, distinctly remember her spooning a touch of Kahlùa over her vanilla ice cream a fair number of times—and every time, she had a big smile on her face as she ate it. I remember her looking so happy. So in honor of her, I created this scrumptious sundae.

½ cup fat-free churned vanilla ice cream
  (I used Breyer's Double Churn)
2 teaspoons chocolate syrup
1½ teaspoons Kahlùa liqueur
1 tablespoon fat-free aerosol whipped
  topping

Spoon the ice cream into a wineglass (a small bowl is okay too). Drizzle the chocolate syrup and Kahlùa evenly over the top. Top with the whipped topping. Serve immediately.

Makes 1 sundae. 155 calories, 4 g protein, 33 g carbohydrates, trace fat, trace saturated fat, trace cholesterol, 3 g fiber, 62 mg sodium

lip-smackin' s'mores sundae

Hands-on Time: 4 MINUTES • *Hands-off Time:* NONE

As you'll notice throughout this book, I use very few fat-free products beyond milk, yogurts, and ice creams because I don't think they taste good. So if you haven't tried fat-free ice cream in a while or you've never tried fat-free double churn, it's definitely worth giving it a try. It's come a long way from the fat-free ice cream of even a few years ago.

The marshmallow used in this recipe is an actual sundae topping. If you can't find it easily, sub in marshmallow creme and stir just the tiniest touch of water into it so it's not so thick. You won't need as much to get it spread over the sundae.

If you're having trouble finding fat-free hot fudge, check the labels of all hot fudge at your grocery store. A number of brands make fat-free versions, but some don't say it on the front of the jar.

1 (1/2 cup) scoop churned, fat-free chocolate or chocolate cookies and cream ice cream (I used Breyer's Double Churn)

2 low-fat honey graham crackers (1/2 sheet)

1 tablespoon fat-free hot fudge, warmed

1 tablespoon marshmallow topping (I used Smucker's)

Scoop the ice cream into a sundae dish or small bowl. Divide the sheet of graham crackers into 2 pieces, then crumble them with your fingers as finely as possible over the ice cream. Drizzle the hot fudge and then the marshmallow evenly over the top. Serve immediately.

Makes 1 serving. 250 calories, 4 g protein, 57 g carbohydrates, trace fat, 0 g saturated fat, 0 mg cholesterol, 3 g fiber, 185 mg sodium

chocolate chip banana boat

Hands-on Time: 3 MINUTES •
Hands-off Time: TIME TO PREHEAT OVEN PLUS 6 TO 8 MINUTES

Okay, this recipe is simple, but last year when I told a friend I was going to write this book he said I had to include it. I'd never heard of doing this, nor had a number of my friends. In fact, though I found many friends who made a version including marshmallows over a campfire as a kid, I didn't find one other person who'd actually made this. So I'm guessing that most folks won't have had it before. Trust me; if you like bananas and chocolate, you'll wish you'd tried it sooner!

1 medium (about 7 inches) banana
1 1/2 teaspoons mini chocolate chips

Preheat the oven to 350°F.

Hold the unpeeled banana so the ends point up. Create a pocket by slicing it down the middle about 1/2 inch from one end to 1/2 inch from the other, being sure not to cut all the way through. Place the banana on a small baking sheet, ends still pointing up, and push the ends slightly toward each other to open the banana. Tuck the chocolate chips evenly in the opening. Bake the stuffed banana for 6 to 8 minutes, or until the banana is soft and the chips are mostly melted. Using a fork, gently mash the melted chips into the softened banana. Serve immediately.

Makes 1 serving. 145 calories, 2 g protein, 34 g carbohydrates, 2 g fat, 1 g saturated fat, 0 mg cholesterol, 4 g fiber, 0 mg sodium

caramel apple sundae snack

Hands-on Time: 4 MINUTES • *Hands-off Time:* NONE

Though most caramel apples might be off limits, this sweet snack sure isn't. It's easy to throw together and great any time of the day . . . even for breakfast!

Next time you go to a warehouse or club store, pick up some clear plastic containers with lids. You can make a few of these at a time and store them in your refrigerator for a few days so they're ready when you are.

1/2 cup fat-free artificially sweetened or naturally sweetened apple turnover or apple-flavored yogurt (I used Yoplait)

2 tablespoons low-fat granola without raisins

1/3 cup chopped apple (about 1/2 small apple)

1 1/2 teaspoons fat-free caramel-flavored topping

Spoon the yogurt into a sundae dish or small, deep bowl. Top the yogurt evenly with the apples, followed by the granola. Drizzle the caramel over the top. Serve immediately.

Makes 1 serving. Made with artificially sweetened yogurt: 176 calories, 6 g protein, 37 g carbohydrates, <1 g fat, trace saturated fat, 3 mg cholesterol, 2 g fiber, 146 mg sodium; Made with naturally-sweetened yogurt: 200 calories, 7 g protein, 43 g carbohydrates, <1 g fat, trace saturated fat, 4 mg cholesterol, 3 g fiber, 144 mg sodium

broiled peaches à la mode

Hands-on Time: 4 MINUTES •
Hands-off Time: TIME TO PREHEAT BROILER PLUS 2 TO 4 MINUTES

I've never appreciated pies the way I know a lot of other folks do. I love chocolate so much that I always feel if I'm going to eat something fattening, I want it to be super-decadent—and pies, to me, are not. If I'm going to eat something that tastes like fruit, I figure I might as well just eat fruit and save the additional calories to later get my chocolate fix. Then I started cooking fruit more, and it totally changed my view. Granted, I make fruit much cleaner (as in healthier) than putting it in pies, but there's something really satisfying about a baked peach or a roasted grapefruit that just doesn't come across in uncooked fruit.

This makes a hearty amount, so it's perfect for when you're craving something sweet, and lots of it. If you want just a little something, I'd recommend sharing it with a buddy.

Butter-flavored cooking spray
2 firm medium peaches
2 tablespoons brown sugar, packed
4 pinches ground cinnamon
1 cup fat-free churned vanilla ice cream,
    divided (I used Breyer's Double Churn)

Preheat the broiler. Line a small baking sheet with foil. Lightly mist the foil with spray.

Cut each peach in half, crossing over the stem. Remove the pit. (If the peach is ripe, this should be easy to do with your fingers. If you have trouble, use a spoon to gently dig it out, being careful not to remove too much of the flesh.) Place the peach halves, side by side, cut sides up, in the pan, and sprinkle each with $1/2$ tablespoon brown sugar and a pinch of cinnamon. Broil on high for 2 to 4 minutes, or until the peaches are tender and the sugar begins to bubble and caramelize (brown lightly).

Divide the peaches between 2 dessert bowls and top each with $1/2$ cup ice cream. Serve immediately.

Makes 2 servings. Each serving (2 peach halves with $1/2$ cup ice cream) has: 187 calories, 4 g protein, 45 g carbohydrates, trace fat, trace saturated fat, 0 mg cholesterol, 5 g fiber, 55 mg sodium

ready-for-guests roasted pears

Hands-on Time: 5 MINUTES •

Hands-off Time: TIME TO PREHEAT OVEN PLUS 40 TO 45 MINUTES PLUS
15 MINUTES TO COOL

When coring the pears, make sure you also remove the fibrous portion along the line of the stem. Then, before serving, make sure to let the pears cool until they are just warm or room temperature. The flavor and texture is much richer once they've cooled. In fact, these pears are perfect for a dinner party or an event where food may be sitting out for a bit; the flavor actually gets better as they rest. Keep in mind the cooking time may vary depending on the variety of pear you use. Some are considerably firmer than others, so if the pears don't seem cooked enough after the suggested cooking time below, continue roasting them until they're very tender. It could take up to an additional half-hour if you get a really firm variety.

Butter-flavored cooking spray

2 firm pears (about 6 ounces each), rinsed

2 teaspoons light butter, melted (stick, not tub; I used Challenge Light)

2 tablespoons brown sugar, not packed

2 pinches cinnamon

Preheat the oven to 350°F. Line an 8 × 8-inch baking dish with parchment. Lightly mist the parchment with spray. Crinkle a piece of foil to form a log about 12 inches long, 4 inches wide, and 1 inch in diameter. Set the log in the center of the baking dish.

Cut the pears in half lengthwise. Carefully scoop out the cores and remove the stems. Place the halves on the prepared baking sheet so the tips rest on the log (this is to ensure the pears lay flat so the glaze doesn't drip out during baking). Drizzle the butter evenly over the pears. Then sprinkle the brown sugar, followed by the cinnamon, evenly over the top. Bake for 40 to 45 minutes, or until very tender. Allow the pears to cool until they're just warm or room temperature, about 15 minutes. Serve immediately.

Makes 2 servings. Each (1 pear; 2 halves) serving has: 155 calories, <1 g protein, 37 g carbohydrates, 2 g fat, 1 g saturated fat, 5 mg cholesterol, 6 g fiber, 36 mg sodium

mini chocolate oreo pudding "pies"

Hands-on Time: 4 MINUTES • *Hands-off Time:* NONE

This quick dessert takes pudding to a new level of decadence by making it a little more like a pie featuring cookie crumbs, reminiscent of a chocolate crumb crust, and a touch of whipped topping. Feel free to make this with any flavor pudding. You can even sub in an all-natural pudding, though that will add calories (about 1/3 cup of sugar-free pudding has only 60 calories, while about 1/3 cup of naturally sweetened pudding has 90 calories). Always be sure to read labels.

Numerous friends have reported, after enjoying this recipe, that they love it as is . . . their husbands usually "require" more Cool Whip. If you're making it for your guy or you are a guy, you may want to add a bit more.

4 (106 g each) sugar-free refrigerated chocolate pudding cups (I used Jell-O Brand)

6 reduced-fat chocolate sandwich cookies, crushed (I used reduced-fat Oreos)

4 tablespoons fat-free frozen whipped topping, defrosted

Divide the crushed cookies evenly among 4 (about 3^1/$_2$-inch-diameter) ramekins or glass bowls. Spread the crumbs in an even layer in the bottom of each ramekin. Spoon one pudding cup over each of the cookie "crusts." Top each with 1 tablespoon whipped topping. Serve immediately.

Makes 4 servings. S Each (1 pie) serving has: 143 calories, 3 g protein, 29 g carbohydrates, 4 g fat, 2 g saturated fat, 0 mg cholesterol, 2 g fiber, 268 mg sodium

cinnamon sugar triangles

Hands-on Time: 5 MINUTES • *Hands-off Time:* 4 TO 5 MINUTES

Be sure to buy eggroll wrappers—the ones that are bigger than wonton skins—to make these triangles. These are an awesome treat at the end of an Asian-inspired meal . . . or any time. Use different colors of decorative sugar to make them extra fun and festive. I love making them with Wilton Sprinkles Pink & White Sparkling Sugar when girlfriends are coming over or when working with the young girls I mentor.

If you want to make these triangles for a group, don't worry. The recipe is really easy to multiply. I was tempted to write the recipe in a larger quantity. But I find them so addicting, I think it's slightly "dangerous" to have them sitting around.

Butter-flavored cooking spray

1/4 teaspoon ground cinnamon

1 tablespoon plus 2 teaspoons raw sugar or coarse colored sugar

2 (7-inch) eggroll wrappers (look for them in the refrigerated section with other international foods at your local grocery store)

1 tablespoon light butter, melted (stick, not tub; I used Challenge Light)

Preheat the oven to 400°F. Lightly mist a large nonstick baking sheet with spray.

In a small bowl, combine the cinnamon and sugar.

Lay the eggroll wrappers side by side on a cutting board. Using a pastry brush, very lightly brush one side of one of the wrappers with half the melted butter, all the way to the edges. Then, sprinkle half the cinnamon-sugar mixture evenly over the butter. Using a pizza cutter, cut the wrapper across both diagonals to create 4 triangles. Repeat with the remaining eggroll wrapper, butter, and cinnamon-sugar. Lay the triangles side by side on the prepared baking sheet so they do not touch. Bake them for 4 to 5 minutes, or until the triangles are crisp and golden brown. Serve immediately, or allow them to cool and store them in an airtight container for up to 1 week.

Makes 8 crisps. Each (2-crisp) serving has: 61 calories, <1 g protein, 11 g carbohydrates, 2 g fat, <1 g saturated fat, 5 mg cholesterol, trace fiber, 54 mg sodium

crunchy bananas & caramel

Hands-on Time: 3 MINUTES • *Hands-off Time:* NONE

Ideally, this recipe should be prepared with firm bananas: The softer ones are best reserved for banana breads and muffins. I buy a couple of bananas pretty much every time I go to the grocery store (way more frequently than most, I'm sure), so I'm always set no matter what I want to do with them.

1 tablespoon fat-free caramel-flavored
   sundae topping
1 small (6 to 7 inches) banana, sliced into
   $1/2$-inch rounds
$1^1/2$ teaspoons high-fiber, low-fat crunchy
   cereal (I used Grape-Nuts)

Heat the caramel sauce in a small bowl in the microwave until warmed, 10 to 30 seconds. Place the bananas in a small, deep bowl. Drizzle the caramel sauce over the bananas. Top evenly with the cereal. Serve immediately.

Makes 1 serving. 170 calories, 2 g protein, 43 g carbohydrates, trace fat, trace saturated fat, 0 mg cholesterol, 4 g fiber, 98 mg sodium

simpler s'mores

Hands-on Time: 3 MINUTES • *Hands-off Time:* NONE

When you go to the grocery store looking for fat-free hot fudge, be sure to flip the jar and look at the nutrition label even if the front doesn't say it's fat-free. Several common brands don't brag about being fat-free, but they are. The store brand at my local grocery store is one of them, so you might want to check at yours.

Feel free to microwave these for a few seconds after you spread each side but before assembling. You'll end up with an even gooier treat!

1 sheet (4 crackers) low-fat honey graham crackers

1½ tablespoons marshmallow creme

1 teaspoon fat-free hot fudge

Break the graham cracker in half to form two squares. Spread the marshmallow creme evenly over the back of one of the squares. Spread the hot fudge over the back of the other square. Put the graham cracker halves together, forming a sandwich, so the marshmallow and hot fudge are in the center. Serve immediately.

Makes 1 serving. 107 calories, 1 g protein, 24 g carbohydrates, <1 g fat, 0 g saturated fat, 0 mg cholesterol, <1 g fiber, 125 mg sodium

gooey gramwiches

Hands-on Time: 2 MINUTES • *Hands-off Time:* NONE

Years ago, I used to make these gramwiches all the time. Every time, my ex-boyfriend, Kyle, would watch the marshmallow as it gooed out of the cracker when I took a bite. He would say, "You're such a child," with a smile on his face. He didn't like marshmallows, but I know he wished he did because this quick treat always put a smile on my face.

1 low-fat graham cracker sheet (4 crackers), broken in half
1 marshmallow

Place one graham cracker half on a microwave-safe plate. Put the marshmallow in the center of the cracker. Watching carefully, microwave it on low until the marshmallow expands by about one-third of its size, 10 to 15 seconds. Top the marshmallow with the remaining graham cracker half, smooshing it down gently. Serve immediately.

Makes 1 serving. 78 calories, 1 g protein, 17 g carbohydrates, <1 g fat, 0 g saturated fat, 0 mg cholesterol, <1 g fiber, 101 mg sodium

chocolate peanut-bears

These adorable little bears are exceptionally great for kids instead of less nutritious sandwich cookies. You can make plenty ahead of time and store them in an airtight plastic container for whenever they (or you) need a snack in seconds.

12 chocolate Teddy Grahams Graham Snacks
1 1/2 teaspoons all-natural creamy peanut
 butter

Arrange 6 of the bears, flat sides up, on a small plate. Spread the peanut butter evenly among them. Top them with the remaining bears, flat sides down.

Makes 1 (6-sandwich) serving. 118 calories, 3 g protein, 13 g carbohydrates, 6 g fat, 1 g saturated fat, 0 mg cholesterol, 1 g fiber, 93 mg sodium

tropical truffles

Hands-on Time: 10 MINUTES • *Hands-off Time:* NONE

Let's face it, baking cookies or making candy can take a lot of time—time we sometimes just don't have. But we do still want to offer treats that are made with love. These truffles are a simple, fast, and fun answer that will keep you from slaving over a stove and will keep your family fit and happy. In fact, they're the perfect homemade sweet treat to impress everyone whether they're interested in eating healthfully or not. And, they're even perfect for getting the kids in the kitchen with you.

1 (5-ounce) bag of dried mangoes, cut into
    1-inch pieces
¼ cup marshmallow creme
⅔ cup old-fashioned oats
¼ cup sweetened flake coconut

Put the mangoes in the bowl of a food processor fitted with a chopping blade and process until the pieces are extremely fine and very sticky. Add the marshmallow creme and coconut and continue processing until well combined. Add the oats and process until they are just incorporated (the finished mixture will be sticky to the touch and the "dough" should hold together easily). Remove the blade from the bowl of the food processor and, using your fingers, divide the mixture into 8 equal amounts. Carefully form each into a ball. Serve immediately, or store in an airtight plastic container for up to 2 days.

Makes 8 servings. Each (1-truffle) serving has: 108 calories, 1 g protein, 23 g carbohydrates, 1 g fat, <1 g saturated fat, 0 mg cholesterol, 1 g fiber, 18 mg sodium

sexy strawberry tapenade

Hands-on Time: 5 MINUTES • *Hands off Time:* UP TO 2 HOURS TO CHILL

When strawberries are in season, this recipe is not only extremely affordable, it's amazingly scrumptious. With each bite, you taste fresh strawberries followed by a hit of chocolate that lingers perfectly. I've come to love this recipe as a topping for low-fat whole-grain waffles and low-fat pancakes, as a dip for cinnamon flatbread sticks, and even as a topping for fat-free vanilla or chocolate ice cream.

Whether your strawberries were cold or not when you started preparing this tapenade, it's best to refrigerate it until they are fully chilled after being mashed.

2 cups quartered, trimmed fresh strawberries

2 tablespoons mini semisweet chocolate chips

In a medium mixing bowl, using a potato masher or pastry blender, mash the berries until they are about the consistency of a chunky applesauce. Cover and refrigerate until well chilled, up to 2 hours. Stir in the chocolate chips just before serving.

Makes 4 servings. Each (generous ¼-cup) serving has: 50 calories, <1 g protein, 9 g carbohydrates, 2 g fat, <1 g saturated fat, 0 mg cholesterol, 2 g fiber, 1 mg sodium

strawberry shortcake to go

Hands-on Time: 5 MINUTES • *Hands-off Time:* NONE

This dessert is great to take out the door, to sell at a bake sale (if you store the cups in a tub of ice), or even to just open the refrigerator to. There's just something so much more appealing about food that's ready to go.

Feel free to make this in any resealable plastic container you have sitting around your kitchen. But if you want it to look like it was made by the pros, next time you go to a warehouse or club store, buy 12-ounce clear plastic take-out cups with lids. If you're making a lot, line them up and fill them assembly-line fashion.

If you have a few extra minutes and want the shortcakes to be even more decadent, try following this recipe using the Sexy Strawberry Tapenade (see page 207) instead of plain strawberries—a ¼-cup serving of the tapenade has only 50 calories and 2 grams of fat. Just layer a serving (or two) of the tapenade between the angel food cake and whipped topping in a 12-ounce cup, and you're in for an extra-special treat.

1¼ ounces angel food cake, torn into bite-sized pieces

1 cup sliced strawberries

¼ cup plus 2 tablespoons fat-free frozen whipped topping, defrosted

Add half of the angel food cake to a 12-ounce plastic to-go beverage cup with a lid or to a medium resealable plastic container. Top with half the strawberries, followed by half the whipped topping. Repeat with the remaining cake, strawberries, and whipped topping. Cover and refrigerate for up to 2 days.

Makes 1 serving. 190 calories, 3 g protein, 42 g carbohydrates, <1 g fat, trace saturated fat, 0 mg cholesterol, 4 g fiber, 282 mg sodium

cinnamon & sugar soft pretzel

Hands-on Time: 4 MINUTES •
Hands-off Time: TIME TO PREHEAT OVEN PLUS 5 TO 6 MINUTES

If you're tempted every time you walk by the pretzel stand at the mall, this recipe is for you. I used a pretty small amount of cinnamon in this recipe because I didn't want it to overpower the flavor of the butter and the sugar. If you're a big fan of cinnamon, feel free to use a little more. Since it's virtually calorie-free, it's consequence-free.

1 (about 64 g) frozen soft pretzel (1 g of fat
    or less per pretzel; I used Super Pretzel)
1/4 teaspoon cinnamon, or more to taste
1/4 cup sugar*
1 teaspoon light butter, melted (stick, not tub;
    I used Challenge Light)

Bake the pretzel according to package directions, omitting any salt, in the oven.

Meanwhile, in a medium shallow bowl, stir the cinnamon and sugar.

Brush the melted butter evenly over both sides of the cooked pretzel, then dip the pretzel in the bowl with the cinnamon-sugar mixture. Flip it and completely coat both sides with the cinnamon-sugar. (Not all of the sugar will be used.) Serve immediately.

Makes 1 serving. 210 calories, 5 g protein, 43 g carbohydrates, 3 g fat, 1 g saturated fat, 5 mg cholesterol, 1 g fiber, 162 mg sodium

*Note: These numbers are based on average sugar consumption, not, a full 1/4 cup.

strawberry banana marshmallow
fondue skewers

Hands-on Time: 3 MINUTES • *Hands-off Time:* NONE

This is a great, colorful treat to serve when hosting a girls' night or cocktail hour. It's fun and extremely easy to make in large quantities, since you're just skewering one piece of marshmallow, strawberry, and banana on each skewer.

When buying hot fudge, you may need to read the nutritional information to determine whether or not it's fat-free. Some brands say "fat-free" directly on the label, but others that are may not say so. Just be sure that "0 g fat" is listed on the nutrition label.

2 marshmallows
2 medium strawberries, rinsed and trimmed
2 (1-inch-thick) rounds ripe banana
1 tablespoon fat-free hot fudge, warmed
2 decorative or wooden skewers

Thread 1 marshmallow, then 1 strawberry, and then 1 banana slice on each skewer. Serve immediately with hot fudge for dipping.

Makes 1 serving. 83 calories, 1 g protein, 21 g carbohydrates, trace fat, trace saturated fat, 0 mg cholesterol, 1 g fiber, 17 mg sodium

irish cream hot chocolate

Hands-on Time: 2 MINUTES • *Hands-off Time:* TIME TO BOIL WATER

I love this hot chocolate when I'm hanging out with girlfriends watching movies or playing board games on cold winter nights.

For a more natural alternative, this recipe can be made with an all-natural cocoa (though it will be a bit higher in calories). Just add 1 tablespoon of Bailey's Irish Cream for every 5 ounces of prepared hot cocoa.

1 (8 g) packet fat-free, sugar-free hot cocoa mix (I use Swiss Miss Sensible Sweets Diet—25 calories)
1 tablespoon Bailey's Irish Cream or other Irish cream liqueur
1 tablespoon fat-free aerosol whipped topping

Prepare the cocoa according to package directions, but omit 1 tablespoon of water. Stir in the Irish cream. Top with whipped topping. Serve immediately.

Makes 1 (5-ounce) serving. 76 calories, 2 g protein, 8 g carbohydrates, 3 g fat, 2 g saturated fat, 68 mg cholesterol, 1 g fiber, 178 mg sodium

icy mocha blended

Hands-on Time: 3 MINUTES • *Hands-off Time:* NONE

This is a great recipe if you have a craving for something sweet but don't want to indulge in an overly caloric dessert. With each serving having only 85 calories and 2 grams of fat, you can save yourself the trip and the cost of going to a coffee shop with a friend and indulge right in your own kitchen.

1 cup low-fat chocolate milk (should be 3 g of fat or less per 1-cup serving)
1 teaspoon instant coffee granules
1 cup (about 9 medium) ice cubes
2 tablespoons fat-free aerosol whipped topping

Add the milk, coffee granules, and ice cubes to the jar of a blender with ice-crushing ability. Blend on high or the ice crush setting until the mixture is smooth and frothy. Divide evenly between 2 glasses, and top each with 1 tablespoon whipped topping. Serve immediately.

Makes 2 servings. Each (8-ounce) serving has: 85 calories, 4 g protein, 17 g carbohydrates, 2 g fat, 1 g saturated fat, 8 mg cholesterol, trace fiber, 112 mg sodium

orange chocolate milkshake

Hands-on Time: 4 MINUTES • *Hands-off Time:* NONE

Though this shake isn't as thick as some, it's still incredibly rich and really satisfies that choco-late craving. In the evening, I love to add Triple Sec or orange liqueur to make it even more indulgent. The liqueur really adds even more depth and makes the shake something special. But either way, I'm sure you'll find it delicious!

3/4 cup churned, fat-free chocolate ice cream
(I used Breyer's Double Churn)
3/4 cup frozen mango cubes
3/4 cup 100% orange juice (not from
concentrate)
1 ounce Triple Sec or orange liqueur, optional

Add the ice cream, mango, orange juice, and Triple Sec (if using) to the jar of a blender with ice-crushing ability. Make sure the lid is on tight. Using an ice crush setting, blend the ingredients until they are relatively smooth, about 1 minute. Then blend on the liquefy or the high speed setting for about 10 seconds until the mixture is completely smooth. Serve immediately.

Makes 2 servings. Each (about 8-ounce) serving has: 158 calories, 3 g protein, 39 g carbohy-drates, 0 g fat, 0 g saturated fat, 0 mg cholesterol, 5 g fiber, 41 mg sodium

slimming banana smoothie

Hands-on Time: 5 MINUTES • *Hands-off Time:* NONE

When looking for the perfect banana for a smoothie, you want to choose one that is not green but also not overly ripe (a few brown spots are great, but you don't want it to be brown). Green bananas are difficult to blend smoothly in the blender and won't give you the nice sweetness ripe bananas will. But, if they're overly ripe, the flavor will be overpowering.

If you're a big fan of smoothies, it's best to buy bananas in bulk when they're on sale. When they are the perfect ripeness, peel them and store them in resealable freezer bags in the freezer so they're ready for you whenever the craving strikes.

1 medium, peeled frozen banana
¼ cup fat-free milk
½ teaspoon vanilla
4 medium ice cubes

Break the banana into 3 or 4 pieces and add it to the jar of a blender with ice-crushing ability along with the milk, vanilla, and ice cubes. Blend on high or the ice crush setting until smooth. Serve immediately.

Makes 1 (8 to 10-ounce) serving. 141 calories, 3 g protein, 33 g carbohydrates, trace fat, trace saturated fat, 1 mg cholesterol, 4 g fiber, 36 mg sodium

the basics

basic grilled chicken

Hands-on Time: 5 MINUTES •
Hands-off Time: TIME TO PREHEAT GRILL PLUS 10 MINUTES

I almost always have Basic Grilled Chicken on hand in my refrigerator. Not only is it great for adding to salads, it makes it a cinch to make nachos, pizzas, and so much more. Plus, it's great cubed when I just get the munchies and want something healthy to snack on.

1 pound trimmed boneless, skinless chicken breast
1 teaspoon extra virgin olive oil
Salt, preferably sea salt, to taste
Pepper, to taste (preferably, fresh ground)

Preheat a grill to high heat. Toss the chicken breasts with the olive oil and season both sides with salt and pepper. Grill the chicken until it is no longer pink inside, about 5 minutes per side.

Makes 4 servings. Each serving has: 135 calories, 26 g protein, 0 g carbohydrates, 3 g fat, 1 g saturated fat, 66 mg cholesterol, 0 g fiber, 74 mg sodium

southwest basic grilled chicken

Hands-on Time: 5 MINUTES •
Hands-off Time: TIME TO PREHEAT GRILL PLUS 10 MINUTES

This chicken is excellent to have on hand if you're as huge a fan of Mexican cuisine as I am. Add it to salad, soups, Southwest wraps, and more. If you use just a touch of salt along with a salt-free Mexican or Southwest seasoning, it will have a ridiculously small fraction of the sodium of any taco, burrito, or fajita seasoning I've seen in grocery stores, not to mention far fewer preservatives.

1 pound trimmed boneless, skinless chicken breast
1 teaspoon extra virgin olive oil
2 teaspoons salt-free Mexican seasoning or rub (I used Southwest Chipotle Mrs. Dash)
Salt, to taste

Preheat a grill to high heat. Toss the chicken breast with the olive oil and season both sides with seasoning and salt. Grill the chicken until it is no longer pink inside, about 5 minutes per side.

Makes 4 servings. Each serving has: 135 calories, 26 g protein, 0 g carbohydrates, 3 g fat, 1 g saturated fat, 66 mg cholesterol, 0 g fiber, 74 mg sodium

simple grilled london broil

Hands-on Time: 4 MINUTES •
Hands-off Time: 15 MINUTES TO REST PLUS 8 to 10 MINUTES PLUS
10 ADDITIONAL MINUTES TO REST

This recipe is a great one to make on a Sunday night. Not only will you have a great dinner, you'll have leftovers (unless, of course, you have a large family, in which case I suggest you make two at the same time) to slice thinly for use as deli meat or to cube for use in salads. It'll have a lot less sodium and less processing than most deli meats you'd buy at your grocery store, and it's much less expensive.

Though I always love the flavor an outdoor grill provides, as a second option, this dish can be prepared under a broiler for 4 to 5 minutes per side for medium-rare, or longer until desired doneness is reached.

1/2 teaspoon sea salt, or to taste
1/2 teaspoon fresh ground black pepper, or to taste
1/2 teaspoon onion powder
1/4 teaspoon garlic powder
1 3/4 pounds trimmed London broil
1 teaspoon extra virgin olive oil

In a small bowl, mix the salt, pepper, and onion and garlic powders until well combined. Rub the meat evenly on all sides with the olive oil, followed by the seasoning mixture.

Preheat a grill to high heat.

Let the meat stand for 15 minutes.

Grill the meat for 4 to 5 minutes per side for medium-rare or longer until desired doneness is reached. Transfer it to a serving platter and cover it loosely (just the meat, not the platter) with a piece of foil. Allow it to rest for 10 minutes, and then slice it thinly against the grain. Serve immediately. Refrigerate any leftovers for up to 3 days.

Makes 6 servings. Each (about 4-ounce) serving has: 137 calories, 28 g protein, trace carbohydrates, 5 g fat, 2 g saturated fat, 58 mg cholesterol, trace fiber, 198 mg sodium

steamed shrimp

I always keep shrimp in my freezer. I buy it in bulk or when it's on sale so it's there when I want it. Shrimp is a great source of lean protein and one of the few proteins you can easily defrost in minutes and without affecting quality. Simply run the frozen shrimp under cold water until it thaws.

This recipe technically makes boiled, not steamed, shrimp. The result is similar, but I have found boiling to yield more consistent results.

1⅓ pounds large (21-25 count or similar) unpeeled shrimp, or 1 pound peeled

Salt, preferably sea salt

Place a bowl of ice water in the sink. Bring a medium pot of salted water to a boil over high heat. Add the shrimp and cook them 1 to 2 minutes until the outsides turn pink and they are cooked through.

Drain the shrimp and transfer them immediately to the bowl of ice water. Drain them again. Peel and eat them immediately, or store them in an airtight plastic container in the refrigerator for up to 3 days.

Makes 4 servings. Each (about 4-ounce) serving has: 120 calories, 23 g protein, 1 g carbohydrates, 2 g fat, trace saturated fat, 172 mg cholesterol, 0 g fiber, 168 mg sodium

brown rice

Hands-on Time: 2 MINUTES •
Hands-off Time: TIME TO BOIL WATER PLUS 40 MINUTES TO SIMMER
PLUS 5 MINUTES TO REST

Brown rice is a must-have staple for healthy eaters. I used to think I wasn't a fan—and then I was introduced to short-grain brown rice (long- and medium-grain varieties are much more commonly found but not nearly as tasty, if you ask me). The short-grain has a nuttier taste that I've truly come to crave. If you haven't tried it, it's definitely time to do so.

One of the best things about brown rice is that you can make a pot on Sunday and it keeps all workweek if refrigerated in an airtight plastic container or resealable plastic bag.

2 cups water
1 cup brown rice (I prefer short-grain)
Salt, to taste

Bring the water to a boil in a medium saucepan over high heat. Stir in the rice and reduce the heat to low. Cover the pan and simmer the rice for 40 minutes. Remove the pan from the heat and allow to stand for 5 minutes. Fluff the rice with a fork. Serve immediately, or allow to cool and refrigerate in a resealable plastic container or plastic bag for up to 5 days.

Makes 4 servings. Each (½-cup) serving has: 109 calories, 2 g protein, 23 g carbohydrates, <1 g fat, trace saturated fat, 0 mg cholesterol, 2 g fiber, <1 mg sodium

hard-boiled egg whites

Hands-on Time: 3 MINUTES •
Hands-off Time: TIME TO BOIL WATER PLUS 13 MINUTES

I love to have egg whites on hand at all times.

A whole large egg white has only 17 calories and no fat, so they're great right out the refrigerator any time of day, whether as part of a meal or for the munchies. I just sprinkle them with a bit of sea salt and fresh cracked pepper or one of my favorite rubs, and they're good to go.

Put 6 to 10 eggs in a medium saucepan with a lid. Pour in enough water to cover them by 1 inch. Bring the water to a boil over high heat. Cover the saucepan and turn the heat to low. Cook the eggs for 13 minutes. Immediately drain them and fill the saucepan with ice, and then run cold water over them; the water should quickly turn ice-cold. If it does not, add more ice. As you peel the eggs, run them under cold water so the shells remove easily. Remove the shells and discard the yolks. Refrigerate any remaining eggs in a resealable plastic container (in or out of the shell) for up to 3 days.

1 egg white has, 17 calories, 4 g protein, trace carbohydrates, 0 g fat, 0 g saturated fat, 0 mg cholesterol, 0 g fiber, 55 mg sodium

easier-than-caramelized onions

Hands-on Time: 5 MINUTES • *Hands-off Time:* 20 TO 22 MINUTES

Caramelized onions are a great accompaniment to many dishes, but I never order them out because they're almost guaranteed to be doused in oil or butter. Here, I make them much lighter but still get that to-die-for flavor I love so much (and you likely will too).

2 medium onions (any variety; about 1¼ pounds), very thinly sliced
2 teaspoons extra virgin olive oil
Sea salt and pepper, to taste

Preheat the oven to 450°F. Line a large baking sheet with parchment paper.

Place the onions on the baking sheet. Drizzle the olive oil over them and season them with salt and pepper. Toss them well. Spread them evenly over the baking sheet. Bake them for 20 to 22 minutes, turning about every 5 minutes, until the onions are cooked through and caramelized (soft and lightly browned).

Makes 4 servings. Each (¼-cup) serving has: 35 calories, trace protein, 3 g carbohydrates, 2 g fat, trace saturated fat, 0 mg cholesterol, <1 g fiber, 1 mg sodium

INDEX